Management of
Cerebral Palsy

Management of Cerebral Palsy

A Transdisciplinary Approach

Kate Tebbett

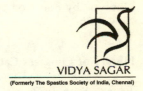

VIDYA SAGAR
(Formerly The Spastics Society of India, Chennai)

Skillshare International

India

SAGE Publications
New Delhi • Thousand Oaks • London

First published in 2006 by

Sage Publications India Pvt Ltd
B-42, Panchsheel Enclave
New Delhi 110 017
www.indiasage.com

Sage Publications Inc
2455 Teller Road
Thousand Oaks, California 91320

Sage Publications Ltd
1 Oliver's Yard, 55 City Road
London EC1Y 1SP

Published by Tejeshwar Singh for Sage Publications India Pvt Ltd, phototypeset in 10.5pt Palatino Linotype by Star Compugraphics Private Limited, Delhi and printed at Chaman Enterprises, New Delhi.

Library of Congress Cataloging-in-Publication Data

Tebbett, Kate, 1972–
    Management of cerebral palsy: a transdisciplinary approach/Kate Tebbett.
      p. cm.
    Includes bibliographical references and index.
    1. Cerebral palsy—Treatment. I. Title.
    [DNLM: 1. Cerebral Palsy—rehabilitation—India. 2. Patient-Centered Care—methods—India. 3. Patient Care Team—India. 4. Quality of Life—India. WS 342 T254m 2006]

    RC388.T33   616.8'36—dc22   2006   2006001077

ISBN: 0-7619-3397-2 (PB)   81-7829-550-4 (India-PB)

Sage Production Team: Anshu Dogra, Ritu Vajpeyi-Mohan, Ashok R. Chandran
                      and Santosh Rawat

Contents

Rationale for this Book

The book documents the experiences of Transdisciplinary working by the staff of Vidya Sagar, Tamil Nadu, south India. In doing so, the book aims at promoting discussion surrounding the current model of medical service provisions for children with special needs and their families, and why this may fail to meet the needs of these children and their families.

The book describes one possible model of working that was developed and implemented by the team at Vidya Sagar. Case studies are included to illustrate how this model changes the intervention these families receive and how the outcome is affected by the change in approach.

Foreword

It is exciting that the first publication documenting the work at Vidya Sagar is ready. Vidya Sagar (formerly The Spastics Society of India, Chennai) has been working in the area of multiple special needs for nineteen years. For many years, we have had a sense of guilt that we are perhaps losing many valuable experiences and lessons learnt in being so action oriented. We have tried to improve our documentation and record keeping but it remains an area of concern.

Kate Tebbett has filled that big void by painstakingly working on this book and documenting at least one of our programmes, the Transdisciplinary Workers' Training.

This has been a valuable experience. Kate is the one who started the project as a physiotherapist and volunteer at Skillshare and it is very appropriate that she should spend the last year and a half in documenting it. Our other trainers from Skillshare have been Ruth Duncan and Rachel Strang.

This entire work would not have been possible without the partnership of Skillshare International (Formerly Action Health, Cambridge, UK). Once they agreed with the concept the team at Action Health, specially Robin Greenwood and Katherine Trott, worked very hard to find the appropriate person. Skillshare first sent a therapist to work with the concept and a curriculum which would take three years to developed. The therapist had a good understanding of India's needs and came up with an excellent project. It took Action Health over a year to finally identify a physiotherapist who agreed with this concept. Kate Tebbett came to our centre in November 1999.

In this book she describes in detail the planning and evolution of the training programme. A year later when Rachel and Ruth joined, many new dimensions were added. Working with our senior special educators has been a very productive and profitable experience for them. The Skillshare volunteers' team finally produced a core of people with excellent Transdisciplinary skills and a curriculum to run a course for the rest of our staff and offer it to other organisations as well.

Kate, Ruth and Rachel very quickly became part of the Vidya Sagar family. They got to know all the children, their parents and all the staff and were always willing to help in the best way possible.

Kate met Jeremy while she was doing the training programme. The first time I met Jeremy I was thrilled because I knew that now we had Kate here in India for a long, long time to come. She stayed with us for four years instead of one. She also made a family for herself and had two children, Sean and Greg.

Ruth Duncan became Ruth Patil when she married Anil. Anil is an Indian and also a development worker. This brought Ruth closer to Vidya Sagar too. Vidya Sagar is also a partner of Basic Needs where Anil worked. Ruth and Anil had Asha, a baby girl.

Rachel came to India with her husband and also went ahead and planned her first baby. Just to say the Transdisciplinary experience was productive in more ways than one!

Skillshare was a huge and constant support; in fact this book came about as a suggestion from Julie George, Development Officer, India.

This book, I hope, will put into perspective the role of the professional rehabilitation worker in the context of the understanding of disability today. Now we are moving towards mainstreaming and inclusion. This book should answer the needs of the social model of disability, where rehab workers must focus on life roles of disabled persons and also draw up intervention and support plans in partnership with disabled people and their families.

The Transdisciplinary worker concept is a step in the direction of supporting main-stream education and increasing support in places where none exists.

This book, I hope, will help all of us in the disability sector to take our debate, dialogue and concerns forward.

Poonam Natarajan
Director, Vidya Sagar

Message

Long before 2000 and the merger of Skillshare Africa and Action Health—two development organisations working in India—Poonam Natarajan embarked upon the mission that led to the birth of her innovative organisation, Vidya Sagar (Ocean of Knowledge) and this seminal book.

Despite losing her only son to the complications of cerebral palsy in 1999, Poonam's unwavering energy and efforts have persisted since 1979 and have finally won credit and academic status for the new Transdisciplinary approach (I don't think we can claim that Poonam invented the idea of Transdisciplinary approach, it has been described by many other people, but she has developed the idea of a Transdisciplinary worker), ensuring its longevity. I'd personally like to congratulate her on her pioneering work.

Since 2000 Skillshare International has enjoyed working in partnership with Vidya Sagar, placing health trainers who have themselves trained a core group of staff and health educators, and we look forward very much to continuing our positive partnership in the future. The role played by our health trainers—Rachel Strang, Ruth Duncan Patil and Kate Tebbett—in giving final shape to the course curriculum on the Transdisciplinary approach is commendable. Katie also took on the extended assignment with us to document the process through the development and application stages of this new approach, from which this book has evolved.

I'd also like to express appreciation to the teams at SAGE for supporting the initial transcript and extending their publishing expertise to this book.

I hope this important book is well received by students, trainers, practitioners and families alike, all united in the struggle to best help children and adults affected by cerebral palsy and the associated multiple disabilities.

Cliff Allum
Chief Executive Officer, Skillshare International

Skillshare International's Vision

Skillshare International's vision is of a world without poverty, injustice, and inequality where people, regardless of cultural, social and political divides, come together for mutual benefit, living in peaceful co-existence.

Introduction

The Transdisciplinary approach to working with people with disabilities as a concept has been described and discussed by many professionals working in the field of disability.

One definition of the concept is:

A Transdisciplinary approach requires the team members to share roles and systematically cross discipline boundaries. The primary purpose of this approach is to pool and integrate the expertise of the team members so that more efficient and comprehensive assessment and intervention services may be provided. The communication style in this type of team involves continuous give and take between all members (especially with the parents) on a regular planned basis. Professionals from different disciplines teach, learn and work together to accomplish a common set of intervention goals for a child and her family. The role differentiation between disciplines is defined by the needs of the situation rather than by discipline specific characteristics. Assessment, intervention and evaluation are carried out jointly by designated members of the team. This teamwork usually results in a decrease in the number of professionals who interact with the child on a daily basis (Bruder 1994).

From reviewing the literature on the subject it becomes evident that a variety of models of working in the way can be explored. It is argued by Millie Smith in *Joseph's Coat: People Teaming in Transdisciplinary Ways* that partial implementation of the concept is more realistic and probably as effective as a more idealistic application of the concept.

The essence of the concept, however it may be applied, is that services to the individual with multiple disabilities should be integrated.

This book is a documentation of our experiences of Transdisciplinary working in Tamil Nadu, south India. The model described in this book includes the development of a professional to be called a 'Transdisciplinary worker'. The book is intended to be read sequentially in order to follow the development of the whole idea, from initial experiences in the field of disability to the eventual training of Transdisciplinary workers.

The development of a Transidsiplinary worker came about as a result of the personal experiences of Poonam Natarajan, a mother of a child with cerebral palsy, who then went on to become a professional in the field of disability. Both her personal and professional experiences led her to the conclusion that one individual trained in special education and all the relevant areas of therapy would be beneficial to both the child and its caregiver. This one individual would be able to look at a child more holistically and give more relevant integrated care. There would also be the benefit that the child, parent or caregiver would need to relate to only one professional on a regular basis.

From this seed of thought, a three-year long training project began at Vidya Sagar (formerly Spastics Society of India, Chennai), whereby a team of six special educators were trained in physiotherapy, speech therapy and occupational therapy for children with special needs. This team became the first Transdisciplinary workers who then went on to develop a course of their own, covering all three areas of therapy. At a later date they also included special education.

The bulk of this book will be the experiences of those people involved in the project, the team at Vidya Sagar, the Action Health Trainers placed by Skillshare International UK, and also the families that the Transdisciplinary workers now work with.

As Transdisciplinary working is not a new treatment method in itself, but a change in approach and a new model of working, the treatment methods themselves will not be described in detail. The treatment methods used in this model are along the lines of normal developmental therapy, but it is the way in which all the elements of the child's needs are integrated in their programme that is different.

This is not the documentation of a research paper and the results are neither qualitative nor quantitative, but we hope that you find this book about our work interesting and can begin to understand what we believe to be the relevance of Transdisciplinary workers in a developing country such as India. We are also keen that this book should encourage further discussion around the need for developing the acceptance of the concept of Transdisciplinary workers, and therefore the need to train more of these individuals.

Part I
Life is for Living

The Importance
of the Family

Experiences of a mother

Poonam Natarajan and her husband Natoo became
parents of Ishoo, a child with special needs, namely
cerebral palsy, in 1979. Poonam remembers that she
was in fact working as a Transdisciplinary worker

from the very beginning. Ishoo needed physiotherapy, speech therapy, occupational therapy and visual training. Finding time to fit in all the programmes set by the different professionals involved in Ishoo's care at this time was impossible!

> I remember the first time I had a big hassle with all the therapy. It was when someone told me they would make out a daily time-table for me every day! I was so angry, I thought I had lost all my freedom!
>
> – Poonam

As Ishoo's mother, Poonam found it hard to separate out his needs as the medical team were doing. Ishoo was her child and a member of the family. Obviously he had a lot of needs, and Poonam and Natoo needed advice on how to handle him, as they wanted to do their best. However, their experiences with the medical team were at times confusing and conflicting, due to poor explanations from professionals as to why a particular piece of furniture was necessary or given to be directly applied to activities of daily living.

> That's one thing with these professionals working with these families. They sometimes forget the social emotional bit of it—which can actually link all of it. It is important that the parent isn't just DOING something all the time. They should be carrying on with daily activities which is what it is all about
>
> – Rajul

In addition, the health professionals would very often be in different parts of the hospital, if not the town, and it was time consuming, to say the least, to get from one person to the other in order to attend all the various appointments.

> The whole experience was very enervating. At this time in your life when you are so emotionally fragile, your relationship with your husband is strained because of having a child with special needs, and on top of this you have to try and build relationships with all these different health professionals... And then the therapists change over so frequently and you have to start all over again! It is emotionally exhausting!
>
> – Poonam

Your complete timetable and instructions for the week,
Mrs Natarajan. It's all there, I think.

From early on Poonam felt it would be so much better to have one person who could answer all your questions, help apply the therapy to your daily routine and, most importantly, facilitate you and others in the family to interact naturally with your child. Consequently, even before Poonam had any professional experience of working in the field of disability she began developing a fully integrated programme for Ishoo, trying to address his various needs during the day as she took care of him as his mother.

Experiences of a professional

In 1981, Poonam trained as a special educator, and in June 1982, she began working at the Spastics Society of Northern India in Delhi.

After moving to Chennai at the end of 1984, Poonam could not find a school that would take her son as a student due to his profound disability. Not disheartened, four months later Poonam started a school in her garage called the Spastics Society of India

Madras, a branch of the Bombay Spastics Society. They began with three children and two staff—Poonam and an occupational therapist.

Within ten months they had grown from providing mainly home management programmes to also running an actual day centre. They now had forty-five children and seven staff. The staff comprised of two special educators, an occupational therapist, a speech therapist, a therapy assistant, and two people for administration and accounts. The school now needed to move out of the garage.

As they were still working primarily as a home management centre, with families coming in for assessment and advice, they immediately realised that they could see more children and give better advice to the parents if they taught each other their own skills, so that each person could work individually. Having knowledge in all areas also helped the team to understand where problems overlapped and they could share their experiences with each other, ensuring that management could be more holistic and applicable; a far more satisfying approach for both the members of the staff and the family. The team spent a lot of time together discussing the different families they saw and exchanging ideas on what advice to give. So began the work of the first Transdisciplinary workers.

> We were actually just doing it (Transdisciplinary working) as part of our work—it was very exciting. We were all so energetic and excited about it, we always wanted to learn.
>
> – Poonam

A growing need

As time went on, and therapists came and went, the fact that the team had a holistic knowledge in all areas of therapy made them an extremely valuable resource. Therapists with knowledge of cerebral palsy were hard to find; very often the therapists they interviewed had experience of only a one-hour lecture on cerebral palsy during their four years of training. One reason for this seemed to be that in general, it was perceived that these children could not achieve much and were something of a lost cause—a view Poonam strongly opposes.

Luckily however, Poonam did find therapists who were keen to join the centre and who were willing to learn, and so there were, at times, therapists on the team. Unfortunately though, they often left after two years, as that was the length of experience they needed in order to get work in the US.

Despite this frequent turnover of staff, the centre itself was continuing to grow. The Spastics Society of India Chennai (Madras now had changed its name!) moved to its current location in a purpose built centre in 1996, which now included a day centre, a home management department, an advisory clinic and an adult vocational training centre. In 1998–99, the organisation became independent from the Spastics Society and was re-named Vidya Sagar, meaning 'ocean of knowledge'.

So there were now more children, more staff, but still few therapists. Poonam and her team had realised by this stage that the issue of recruiting therapists was not going to solve itself, and so the concept of a Transdisciplinary worker needed to be developed further.

Feeding? The man who knows about that is in Speech Therapy.
Far end of the corridor, up two flights of stairs.

Vidya Sagar was also gradually taking on more and more community based rehabilitation work. This again highlighted the need for developing professionals capable of carrying out assessments and designing programmes in all areas of therapy as well as special education for a child with special needs. With teams from the centre going out to ten or more rural based programmes on a monthly basis, it was impossible for the whole multidisciplinary team to be sent to all the projects on each trip. This could mean that questions raised by some of the families could go unanswered for several months at a stretch.

As a developing country, the needs of India are different from those of a developed country. With such large numbers living in rural communities, without ready access to the multidisciplinary team, which is usually hospital based, a different model of working is required.

The need for Transdisciplinary workers in a CBR setting may be more immediately obvious. Within a city it can probably easily be argued that with a good multidisciplinary team functioning together in one centre, for example, as happens in what is called in the west a 'child development centre', the need for another professional is questionable.

However, within organisations like Vidya Sagar, which are managing large numbers of children with disabilities, we believe the standard of service will be better if an integrated approach is used.

The role of the multidisciplinary team

It is not that we at Vidya Sagar believe that the multidisciplinary team is not necessary; far from it. However, with the development of Transdisciplinary working the role of the team is different (see diagrams and descriptions Chapter 4).

Many medical conditions affect only one or two systems of the body; therefore individuals only need to have contact with a limited number of health professionals. In contrast, cerebral palsy very often affects several systems in the body. Therefore, these families always have to cope with a large number of hospital appointments and interactions with many different professionals, an experience which Poonam describes personally, and understandably, as emotionally exhausting.

Transdisciplinary working aims to reduce this feeling by giving families one key worker to whom they can address their questions, someone who can answer all their queries. It is this person who refers to others, may go for appointments with the family if the person doesn't have answers, rather than send the parent to numerous other professionals. The person also helps the parents interact more confidently with the medical team.

The role of different therapists and medical teams in this model is then to give more specialist input and advice to the Transdisciplinary workers, who will then develop an appropriate programme for the families they work with.

Another argument in support of the development of Transdisciplinary workers arises from the more recent concept of inclusion that is now being addressed in India. The vision is for all children with special needs to be allowed to attend mainstream schools. As this idea grows, the need for a Transdisciplinary worker will again be relevant. As a class teacher, it will be far easier to have one professional to relate to who can advise on all of a child's particular needs, and this one individual again, can devise a more integrated programme that allows the child to fit more naturally into the classroom, rather than being taken somewhere separately to do all the various therapy or education programmes.

Opposition to the idea

When discussing her idea with others working in similar situations, Poonam did face opposition. Many people were interested but thought it would be a long process to go through. So here we are, after three years of hard work developing a trained team, to tell you about our experiences.

One thought voiced to Poonam when discussing this project was that this approach would be overburdening one person with too much knowledge. A valid point, but having worked as a Transdisciplinary worker herself for many years (although at that time without giving it a name), not to mention her experiences as a mother, Poonam did not agree with this objection to her idea. The team involved in this project will give their feedback on this issue later in the book when describing their experiences.

An important point related to this is that Transdisciplinary workers are not being trained to cover all conditions (respiratory conditions, arthritis, sports injuries, strokes, etc.) that individual therapists have knowledge about. The training is designed purely to enable these people to work with children with special needs.

Poonam believes that by breaking down walls of specialisation, the child can be seen as a child rather than a series of medical conditions.

Another objection was from some of the health professionals, perhaps due to professional defensiveness. Within the medical team there are clear cut boundaries between the different medical professionals and increasing specialisation within the professions themselves. For example, a physiotherapist may specialise to the degree of becoming a hand therapist, respiratory therapist or manipulative therapist. The same may also be said of doctors, occupational therapists and speech therapists. With this degree of specialisation obviously comes the benefit of increased knowledge and expertise. The problem of professional defensiveness arises when the skills of different professionals are taught to someone outside that profession. As the professionals themselves must (will) have spent many years specialising in their respective areas, to then suggest that their knowledge can be condensed and easily passed on to another individual somewhat negates their level of expertise. This is not the intention of anyone involved in this project. The idea is that a basic but thorough introduction be taught that enables the newly trained individual, the Transdisciplinary worker, to assess and plan intervention for a child, but at the same time know one's own limits and be able to refer back to the specialists for very specific advice.

A note on Conductive Education

Conductive Education is obviously another very popular approach to the management of children with cerebral palsy and in some ways the Conductor may be seen as similar to what we are calling a Transdisciplinary worker. The differences primarily are that a Conductor works with children in a group and they follow a single programme together, which is appropriately adapted for each child. The Transdisciplinary worker on the other hand works with each child individually. This is particularly relevant in rural areas where there may only be one or two children in a village with special needs. In this kind of a scenario, the role of a Transdisciplinary worker facilitating inclusion into a mainstream school is critical. Conductive Education also tends to be rather demanding on both parent and child, while Transdisciplinary working aims to integrate the child into the family as easily as possible without adding extra strain to already stressed parents.

Also there is the issue of cost regarding Conductive Education. Conductive Education is not readily available in India; so travel abroad is necessary for parents wishing to pursue this type of management, something that is impossible for many families.

... Our underlying beliefs about management of cerebral palsy ...

- **Individuals should be supported so they are able to achieve their full potential.**
  Professionals should not concentrate on things that these people cannot and may never be able to do, but should let them move on and achieve what they can.

- **The over-riding aim should be to make the quality of life as rich as possible for the student and its family.**
  How do the children feel about their day and about themselves? Are they dreading a life of therapy or looking forward to a life of good experiences?

- **Learning takes place in all sorts of environments, during all sorts of activities.**
  Many children cannot generalise skills they learn in an isolated situation, such as a therapy room. Performance of daily activities should incorporate therapy as far as possible.

- **Facilitate the family to function as a family, not a medical team!**
  They should be enabled to be as natural as possible in their interactions and activities.

- **These children CAN achieve things. Look critically at what matters to these children. What does independence mean to them?**
  This may mean redefining your understanding of the word 'achievement'. For some children it may mean facilitating them to ask for help when they need it, or to make choices about at least some areas of their life.

- **What is the relevance of the therapy that you are doing? Therapy should enhance the child's life.**
  The children and their caregivers should be involved in setting the goals of therapy in order to help them see the relevance of exercises or activities they have to carry out.

- **Professionals working in the field of disability should be willing to share their knowledge and learn from each other.**
  Knowledge is power—sharing knowledge is progress.

- **Children learn from each other as much as they learn from their teacher or therapists.**

- **Good self-esteem is essential for these children to take control over their life.**

- **Life is for LIVING!!! Not treatments!**

2

From Special Educator to Transdisciplinary Worker

Facts and figures

It is well known that India is a large country with an enormous population, which is estimated to be around the 1.2 billion. Within this population there are obviously various groups of individuals who are excluded from society and mainstream development in some way. People with disabilities are just one of these groups. The numbers of disabled people are contested and vary due to differing definitions of disability and the reliability of sample surveys. Although the National Planning Commission uses the figure of 4 per cent for budgetary purposes (only recently increased from 1.9 per cent), the most commonly accepted figure is 6 per cent or 70 million people. India has the largest number of disabled people in the world.

Although there are many therapists trained in India, many of them go overseas soon after they qualify.

To put that into perspective, the number of disabled people in India is the same as the entire population of the UK.

Another important point to consider is the distribution of this population. It is estimated that approximately 80 per cent of the Indian population lives in rural areas, but as most men leave the villages to find work in the cities, the rural population consists mainly of children, women, the elderly and the disabled.

These people have limited access to medical facilities, often limited education and in many cases are resource-poor which further limits their ability to travel for medical advice.

Indian family's perspectives on disability

An important issue worth discussing at this point is the perspectives of Indian families with regard to disability.

In the case of upper and middle class families the pride and honour of the family are linked to its capacity to address the needs of its members Whether it is a young widow or an elderly member with no income or a member with a disability, they are all nobody's concern but that of the family. Social, emotional, financial or other problems of these disabled and/or dependent members are kept within the proviso of the family. Not only because of the stigma attached to it, but also because the family's pride relies on its ability to manage these problems within its own means. On the one hand, credit goes to the family system and its ability to manage a variety of challenges and disabilities by itself, but on the other hand, this very quality of the family has kept the common concerns of the disabled population at the level of 'individual problems'.

In the lower class and lower caste Indian families the scenario is quite different. Here pride and honour have not disguised the real facts of life. In these poor Indian homes, almost all members of the family are engaged in some remunerative activity. Their existence depends on their job, which gets them barely two square meals a day. Each member has to work for existence and 'survival of the fittest' is the governing principle. Under such circumstances, the disabled members are often left to their own fate or, at best, institutional confinement is resorted to as a solution. At this extreme end of the economic spectrum, families do not hesitate to abandon their disabled children, or look for institutional arrangements.

Although the above two scenarios are considerably different, neither adequately addresses the needs of a person with a disability, or in fact looks at that person as someone who has anything to offer to the family. Also worth considering is the fact that although the national average literacy for India is 56 per cent, amongst the disabled it is estimated to be only 25 per cent, with only 8 per cent of India's disabled children in full-time education. Even more significantly, the rate of unemployment amongst the disabled is over 99 per cent.

The Persons with Disabilities Act 1995, which seeks to emphasise rights of equality of access to opportunities and services, and the government policy of 'Education for all' are encouraging the inclusion of people with disabilities both within schools and society. In order to facilitate this further, services to enable people with disabilities to reach their full potential need to be in place.

The concept of a Transdisciplinary worker is aimed at ensuring that a larger number of people with disabilities can be reached more efficiently and with a depth of understanding about neurological disability that enables the needs of these people to be properly understood and addressed.

Vidya Sagar has various departments that offer services to people with special needs, from community based rehabilitation partnerships to city based programmes and advisory clinics for families from anywhere in India.

Community based rehabilitation (CBR)

Many of the special educators and therapists at Vidya Sagar are involved in the community based rehabilitation projects. Each month teams of two or three people from Vidya Sagar go out to rural projects to work alongside and train the local CBR workers. These workers are usually educated till 10th or 12th standard and have then had further training from Vidya Sagar relevant to CBR work.

Generally, there is a partnership between Vidya Sagar and a rural NGO for three years, and during that time the aim is to develop the local CBR workers into resource people for that area. NGOs often work with people who have a range of disabilities. Vidya Sagar is involved in training workers who would be involved in handling children or adults with neurological problems. Even if the Transdisciplinary course were not developed, these CBR workers would have received training in

Many special educators and therapists at Vidya Sagar are involved in CBR projects.

speech therapy, physiotherapy and occupational therapy from the individual professionals at Vidya Sagar. However, due to the time factor, this would have only been a basic introductory training in the different therapies.

> During 2002–3 Vidya Sagar was working with 30 CBR partners within Tamil Nadu, Kerala and Karnataka; 145 of the local CBR workers underwent training at Vidya Sagar and an estimated 15,000 families were reached by these CBR workers.

The teams from Vidya Sagar who visit on a monthly basis are then responsible for giving further advice on individual cases when a CBR worker has doubts and queries. As stated in the previous chapter, it is not possible to send out a full multidisciplinary team to each project every month. Prior to the Transdisciplinary training this meant that very often queries relating to therapy issues could not be answered until the following month when either the special educator could ask advice from someone at Vidya Sagar or a therapist was able to travel to the project.

Although all the special educators had received training in various therapy areas during their Special Education Diploma, they very often lacked experience and confidence to tackle problems arising in these areas. They tended to avoid things they did not fully understand and felt that their assessment skills were limited, which caused difficulties when trying to implement and subsequently to improve a treatment programme.

Limited understanding of technical jargon and terminology often meant that the special educators felt inadequate to query doctors and shied away from matters they did not fully comprehend. Obviously this was not always beneficial to the children.

Out-patients

Within the out-patients department at Vidya Sagar, there is one special educator responsible for the running of the department and carrying out the majority of the assessments. Other members of the staff, either special educators or therapists, also do one or two sessions a week, including carrying out assessments. Prior to the Transdisciplinary training, a great deal of time was spent waiting for the physiotherapist, speech therapist or the occupational therapist to conduct their respective assessments. The special educators themselves were not confident about liasing with doctors, particularly regarding issues such as surgery. This, on occasions, meant that the treatment suggested or carried out by a doctor was not followed up properly, which again led to the children not benefiting fully from intervention. The special educators working in the out-patients department realised that with training in all areas of therapy they would be able to do their job more efficiently and effectively.

Home management

Within the home management department there are special educators, a physiotherapist and a speech therapist; so there has always been someone around to answer doubts and queries. The problem here was that the management programmes for the children tended to be separated out into speech, physio and education. The staff felt that they were often underestimating the children by not observing how their different disabilities influenced each other. They also realised that they were not using their time efficiently, resulting in less children being assessed than possible, and the waiting list growing rapidly. By being trained in all areas of therapy as well as education, each special educator could work holistically with each child.

Day centre

Within the day centre the problems that the special educators faced were related to poor understanding of therapy issues. This meant that they were not always sure of why they were carrying out a particular line of therapy or how to position a child correctly and did not feel confident to communicate their concerns with the therapy teams.

As with the home management department, the programmes for the children were poorly integrated and the prioritisation of the child's needs was not always appropriate. Separation of

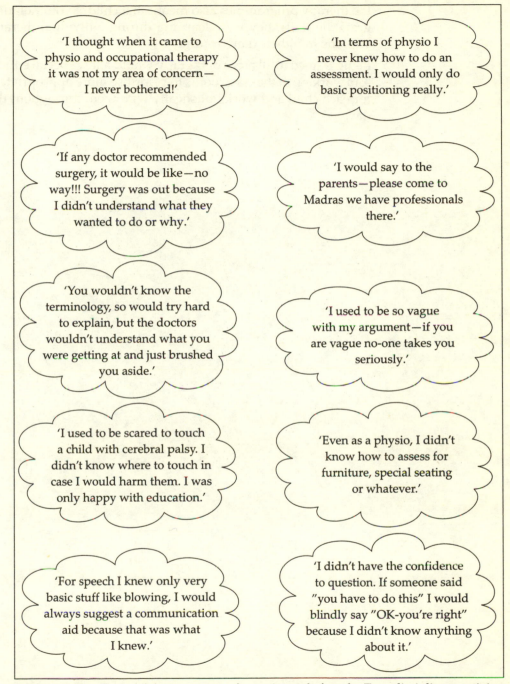

Figure 2.1: Comments of the core team of experiences before the Transdisciplinary training

the therapy programmes also meant that children did not integrate the skills they were learning during individual therapy sessions into their daily routine.

Being trained in all areas of therapy would allow special educators working in the classrooms to prioritise more appropriately for each child and work holistically with them throughout the day.

3 Partnerships with Fellow Organisations

Having discussed her ideas at length with the senior staff at Vidya Sagar, Poonam approached Action Health (which merged with Skillshare Africa in 2000 to become Skillshare International), to form a training partnership. Skillshare International is a UK based charity that forms partnerships with NGOs in developing countries (see appendix for contact address). Their inputs are always aimed at building the capacities of local partners in the government or NGO sector, so that after a set number of months or years, the partnership is no longer necessary, and that the partners can continue developing their institutions and programmes independently.

Skillshare International was to recruit physiotherapists and occupational therapists, as Action Health Trainers, to come to India and train a core team of eight people (see original proposed training curriculum in appendix). Members of this core team would then become competent trainers in physio/occupational therapy assessment and management of children with physical disabilities, particularly neurological disability.

This core team of eight would then go on to develop a sixteen week training module that would be included as an additional optional module to the existing postgraduate diploma course in Special Education already being run at Vidya Sagar. In addition, the core team would also be involved in the training of CBR workers in the areas mentioned above.

Overall, the partnership with Skillshare International would last four years (see Figure 3.1), with the third year seeing the core team running the course that had

Year 1

Core team of eight to be trained by Action Health Trainers. Core team to develop curriculum and training manual.

Year 2

One half of the core team to run the training module on the post-graduate diploma course. The other half of the core team to provide further training for existing staff at Vidya Sagar. Action Health Trainers to support trainers.

Year 3

Core team should be able to run the course independently. Action Health Trainers providing support as necessary.

Year 4

Consolidation of the training programme and making it available to the public.

Figure 3.1 Four-year training in the Transdisciplinary Approach

been developed with back up and input from the Action Health Trainers as required and the final year spent on undertaking an intensive process documentation on the evolution of the Trans-disciplinary approach, which formed the basis for this book.

At the time that the partnership was planned, the Spastics Society of Tamil Nadu was planning to run a course on speech and language therapy, so it was hoped that staff from Vidya Sagar could attend that training in order to increase their knowledge in that area also.

Introducing the core team

Poonam had to select the core team of trainees from her staff. Her criteria were obviously that they should agree with this concept and be motivated to undergo the training. Intelligence and open-mindedness were essential! She also wanted them to commit to staying at Vidya Sagar for several years to complete implementing and consolidating the model of Transdisciplinary working. However, life is unpredictable and those who seemed initially most likely to stay around had to move away due to family commitments during the training itself. Though from the initial nine that were chosen, after three years, there were still six—Mallika, Sudha, Lakshmi, Sadiya, Viji and Priya (see Figure 3.2).

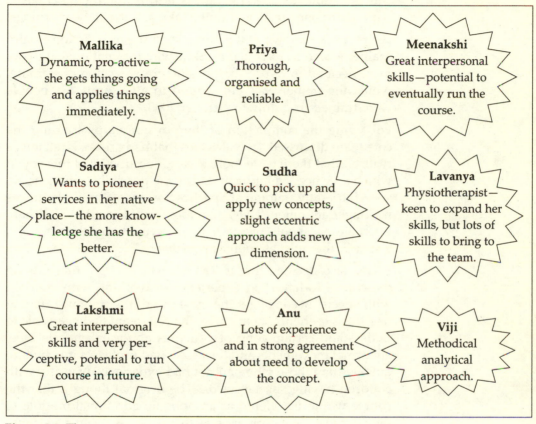

Mallika
Dynamic, pro-active—she gets things going and applies things immediately.

Priya
Thorough, organised and reliable.

Meenakshi
Great interpersonal skills—potential to eventually run the course.

Sadiya
Wants to pioneer services in her native place—the more knowledge she has the better.

Sudha
Quick to pick up and apply new concepts, slight eccentric approach adds new dimension.

Lavanya
Physiotherapist—keen to expand her skills, but lots of skills to bring to the team.

Lakshmi
Great interpersonal skills and very perceptive, potential to run course in future.

Anu
Lots of experience and in strong agreement about need to develop the concept.

Viji
Methodical analytical approach.

Figure 3.2: The core team

The training begins

Skillshare International did not manage to recruit either physiotherapists or occupational therapists as quickly as planned. Their difficulty was finding therapists who were open-minded about this project. The advice from the charitable societies in the UK was along the lines of only undertaking projects that would further the development of the professions, not reduce the role of a professional, as it may have been perceived initially with this project proposal. But finally in November 1999, the first trainer, a physiotherapist, arrived at Vidya Sagar.

Training of the core team began in January 2000 (see appendix for curriculum) and continued until June 2000. The training was part time; lectures taking place three afternoons a week, with one to one practical training taking place in the mornings.

As it was not known at this time when the next Action Health Trainer would be recruited by Skillshare International, the core team decided to re-run the physiotherapy section of training, whilst the trainer was still around to give input. Six people were trained from July to October 2000.

Following the completion of the physiotherapy training the core team discussed several issues that had arisen. First, it was realised that there were more areas of occupational therapy in which they needed input, and also, the possibility of attending speech therapy training at Spastics Society of Tamil Nadu was no longer an option. They, therefore, were keen that Skillshare International should recruit both an occupational therapist and a speech therapist as soon as possible.

It was also decided that it was necessary for participants on the course to have had experience in working with children with special needs to get the most out of the training. Having had this experience themselves, the core team had been able to understand certain concepts, such as abnormal muscle tone, abnormal movements and the associated problems much more quickly than those who had not had experience working with children having special needs. The original thought that the course would be offered as an optional additional module to the post-graduate diploma was therefore reviewed and it was decided that the course would stand on its own and be offered to people who already had at least two years' experience working with children with disabilities.

Fortunately, during August 2000, Skillshare International, recruited both an occupational therapist and a speech therapist. These two therapists were able to commit to part-time training at Vidya Sagar and so it was decided that the occupational therapy component and the speech therapy component would be carried out simultaneously.

This training began in January 2001 and ran until October 2001 (see appendix for curricula), with both lectures and one-to-one practical time.

Once this training was completed, the core team felt they needed time to practice the skills and apply the knowledge they had learned for a few months before they attempted to run a course themselves. However, plans for the Transdisciplinary course began and monthly workshops took place to work on developing the curriculum and structure for the course.

The development of the Transdisciplinary course

When it came to actually planning the Transdisciplinary course, the unanimous opinion was that all elements of therapy should be integrated as much as possible from the start, and teaching the three elements consecutively should be avoided. It was agreed that this would enable future trainees to integrate their understanding and treatment approach right from the start.

How to actually go about this was another matter! The core team were very aware of the quantity of information and knowledge they had gained over the previous two years and were anxious that if the course were not planned carefully enough, it would be very confusing for the trainees, particularly because the plan was to condense the course into a much shorter time frame. At the first planning workshop the core team wrote all the subjects that they had been taught on individual pieces of paper and these were placed on the floor. Following extensive discussions, these subjects were then grouped together where there were common themes, areas of overlap or synergy. This process went on for quite a while as ideas were discussed, reviewed and reorganised, but finally four modules were agreed upon (see Figure 3.3).

The changes in the course content and curriculum occurred gradually over the years as the core team became more experienced themselves. During their training they had realised which areas needed more emphasis and how different subject areas influenced each other and so planned to integrate subjects more when they eventually taught the course. They realised

- **Introductory Module**
  To include the introduction of certain concepts, ideas and philosophies.

- **Anatomy and Physiology**
  To include details on muscles, joints, oral musculature, and the nervous system.

- **Normal Development and Functional Skills**
  To include gross and fine motor development, speech and communication development, and perceptual development.

- **Management**
  To include all modalities of treatment for dysfunction in any of the areas of development as observed in the previous module.

Figure 3.3: Modules of the Transdisciplinary course

that the emphasis should be on function rather than the medical condition and this led to a far more integrated structure for the course.

The concept of life roles

The concept of life roles and how they change in a person's life span was an idea taught to the core team during their occupational therapy training, and one that they had identified with. It was therefore felt that this idea would be a good basis around which to structure the course.

The theory of life roles is based on social psychology and emphasises viewing the child as a person with life roles, not just a medical diagnosis. The theory also recognises the impact of masculine-feminine identification, family, culture, group membership and occupational life roles. Occupational life roles have attributes defining a person's position in society as well as the tasks that he or she must do. The theory looks closely at self-esteem, recognising that this is directly linked to a person's ability to fulfil life roles.

The theory also reflects how a person's life roles change throughout their life span, regardless of whether or not a person has a disability. Looking at an individual in this way facilitates one to examine the issues facing that person from another perspective.

When applying one's underlying beliefs on the management of cerebral palsy (Chapter 1), this approach addresses those beliefs quite clearly.

Let us take for example, Rohini, a teenage girl with ataxia. If one was to look at her from a medical-diagnostic angle, one would identity her problems as having poor balance and coordination and would address these needs in her therapy programme. Though this of course is not incorrect, if one adopts the perspective of life roles, Rohini as a student and as a growing, young person, will see her needs quite differently. She has interests similar to a girl her age as one may easily predict — fashion, shopping, socialising with friends, etc. For her, what is most relevant is being able to do these things. It may be that goals of her treatment include things such as being able to put on her earrings, or to safely negotiate steps into a shop or cinema. Her treatments therefore should reflect these goals, with as much 'therapy' taking place during her daily activities as possible. This is not to suggest, however, that she does not need to do therapy exercises, but with clear goals in mind, hopefully she will see the relevance and her motivation and compliance will be better.

Another example could be Abijit, a teenager with profound disabilities and very dependent on his caregivers for all aspects of his daily care. It is in the context of such children that one may need to think quite carefully about one's definition of achievement. Facilitating ease of care is obviously going to be one goal, recognising that life will be more pleasant for everyone if self-maintenance activities can be carried out as efficiently and as comfortably as possible. But Abijit has other life roles to consider, for example, being part of the family. If he is facilitated to make simple choices so that he can communicate likes and dislikes, he can become a less passive member of the family, enjoying things they may do together, like watching TV, listening to music, having a meal. Another important consideration in this kind of a scenario is facilitating the family to function as naturally as possible. It may involve looking at how to transport the child easily so the family can continue to go out together.

The point with this approach is that, as one can see, we are not trying to introduce new treatment ideas or modalities. We are primarily applying the principles of normal developmental therapy, but from a different perspective. The most important aim is to enhance self-esteem and to promote good relationships within the family.

The Transdisciplinary aspect of management is relevant when trying to understand how the different problems a child may have influence each other. A therapy programme addressing only one area of problems, for example, gross motor problems, will have limited success when there are other elements also affecting the child's performance, for example, perceptual problems. This is when understanding of all areas is helpful in designing an integrated therapy/management programme.

Life roles—enhancement, advancement and maintenance

Trombly's theory basically says that a person's life is made up of roles that fit into the categories of self-maintenance, self-enhancement and self-advancement. Each individual may define his/her roles differently, and those roles may overlap in some areas, but in the centre there is the individual.

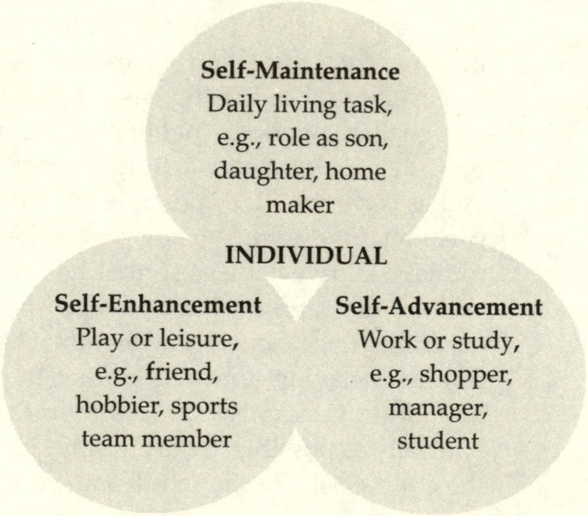

Self-Maintenance
Daily living task,
e.g., role as son,
daughter, home
maker

INDIVIDUAL

Self-Enhancement
Play or leisure,
e.g., friend,
hobbier, sports
team member

Self-Advancement
Work or study,
e.g., shopper,
manager,
student

Figure 3.4: Life roles

Note: *This diagram is our interpretation and application of Trombly's theory.*

Structuring the course

Videos were made of children with normal development to cover all of childhood through to adulthood (see Figure 3.5). These videos showed children in their various life roles—for example, sibling, son or daughter, friend and student—and the skills that they were using or developing during the activities involved in these life roles. The students were given a series of questions to answer while watching each video, covering all areas of the child's development. The lectures in the weeks subsequent to watching each video would then cover the subjects from either the Normal Development and Functional Skills Module, or the Management Module as shown in Figure 3.5. The topics of the lectures were chosen on the grounds of what area of a child's development was most predominant during that age range. For example, during the first year of life the development of movement abilities is high and a child begins to eat solid food as well. This is not to say that the other areas are not developing and it could probably be argued that the lectures could have been carried out in an alternative order. However, this was the order agreed upon by the core team (see appendix–Transdisciplinary Course Content).

The final video showing growth and development from 8 years to adulthood was one of the concluding sessions of the entire course. The reason for this was to highlight how children are learning and developing skills throughout their childhood to enable them to function as an adult. We wanted to bring this idea into the management approach of children with special needs. We hoped this would encourage looking at long-term needs of an individual and their family and therefore make goals and programmes more relevant and realistic.

Goal setting and programme planning will be discussed in more detail in Part II of this book.

The Transdisciplinary course itself was first run over 20 weeks from July 2002 to the beginning of November 2002, on a part-time basis. Lectures took place every afternoon, whilst individual sessions to cover assessments, practicals and mentoring took place in the morning with each trainee having one individual session every week with their mentor.

Age range	Lectures that followed observation of video
0–1 years	Normal posture and movement Normal developmental therapy Positioning Normal sensory development Normal eating/drinking
1–3 years	Development of perception Sensory integration Normal speech and language development Interaction Receptive and expressive language AAC Hearing impairment
3–5 years	Development of hand function Speech Language disorders
5–8 years	Play Automatic and voluntary movement Praxis Normal gait/gait analysis/gait re-education Contracture management
8–35 years	Reflection/discussions/tying up

Figure 3.5: Videos showing normal development from childhood to adulthood

As this course and the whole concept is so new, the content, timing and structure of the course continue to be under review and discussion, with comments and feedback from both trainers and trainees being considered carefully and changes being made as needed.

It is hoped that the process of developing this evolving concept would continue as further batches of students are trained, and interested and related individuals make enquiries or recommendations.

Part II

Individuals Need Support to Achieve Their Full Potential

4

The Transdisciplinary Philosophy

After working for three years to develop the initial idea of calling the professional a Transdisciplinary worker, we came up with our underlying philosophy and the qualities of a Transdisciplinary worker along with the various models of Transdisciplinary working that can be used depending on the setting.

The philosophy

'The whole is more important than the sum of its parts'. An individual with disabilities should be facilitated to become an active member of his/her family and society, fulfilling his/her life roles as far as possible and achieving his/her maximum potential. To minimise the stress of the disability on both the individual and the family, there should be one professional, a Transdisciplinary worker, who is able to assess and develop a management programme for the individual incorporating all areas of his/her life, remembering that the whole is more important than the sum of its parts. The focus should always be on quality of life and promoting self-esteem, essential for helping these people to achieve maximum independence.

Qualities of a Transdisciplinary worker

The Transdisciplinary worker is someone who:

- Has sufficient depth of knowledge in physiotherapy, occupational therapy, speech therapy and special education to assess an individual's needs, and plan and carry out an integrated programme.

- Can use her/his knowledge to support and advise parents.
- Knows her/his own limitations and refers appropriately back to the medical team in the above areas, or senior teach-ing staff for specialist advice and inputs.
- Has a clear understanding of normal development and the concept of life roles, and so can use this as a basis to help a child fulfill these life roles through the management programme.
- Realises the importance of self-esteem for these children and considers this throughout their management.
- Is open minded towards sharing knowledge and skills with other people working in the field of disability.
- Realises the importance of being up-to-date with med-ical progress made in the field of disability, so she/he can play a part in advising families as new treatments become available.

(Note: The main difference between a Transdisciplinary worker and a CBR worker is the level of knowledge. Transdisciplinary workers will have a greater depth of knowledge and a larger repertoire of assessment and treatment ideas. Further, Trans-disciplinary workers are well equipped to work within city en-vironments in a supportive and advisory capacity when a child is integrated into mainstream school.)

The models of Transdisciplinary working

As there are various settings in which children or adults with disabilities are seen by health workers or special educators, there are a few different models illustrating how Transdisciplinary working can take place in each setting.

Home management, out-patients/advisory clinic setting (see Figure 4.1)

In these types of settings the Transdisciplinary worker usually works directly with the child and parent in a one to one situation. The Transdisciplinary worker will be responsible for doing all the assessments (special education, physio, speech and occupational therapy) of the child or adult with disabilities and designing the management programme. The sessions that subsequently take place with the Transdisciplinary worker should, as far as possible, consist of integrated activities, combining the physiotherapy, speech therapy and occupational therapy aspects as well as education. In general, specific therapy exercises that are less easily integrated with other parts of a child's daily routine can be carried out by the Transdisciplinary worker, and taught to the parent or caregiver as appropriate. However, there may be cases where an individual needs specific input from the specialist therapist and, therefore, may receive extra sessions with the relevant member of the multidisciplinary team. The Transdisciplinary worker also teaches the parents treatment skills and helps them work out ways to incorporate therapy into their child's daily routine.

Within this model, it is the Transdisciplinary worker who does the maximum liaising with the multidisciplinary team, asking

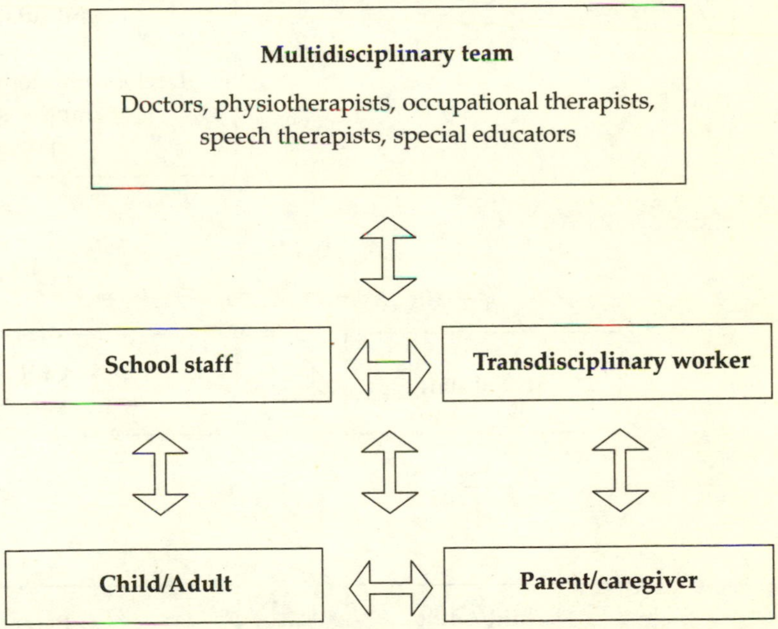

Multidisciplinary team

Doctors, physiotherapists, occupational therapists, speech therapists, special educators

School staff   **Transdisciplinary worker**

Child/Adult   **Parent/caregiver**

Figure 4.1: Transdisciplinary working in home management and outpatients advisory clinic settings

for specific advice, or consulting them on more complex issues, for example, surgical intervention or drug therapy. Should the family need to consult a member of the multidisciplinary team, it is advisable that the Transdisciplinary worker be present, since she/he will have the relevant background about the child, which will assist the multidisciplinary team in deciding the appropriate intervention. The worker will also be able to reassure and explain more complicated terminology and concepts to the parents, who may otherwise feel intimidated in the medical setting.

The Transdisciplinary worker will also have a large role to play in liaising with the school that the child attends regarding the child's needs and the programme being followed.

Community based rehabilitation setting (see Figure 4.2)

In this setting the model is slightly different from the one described earlier in that although the CBR workers themselves function in

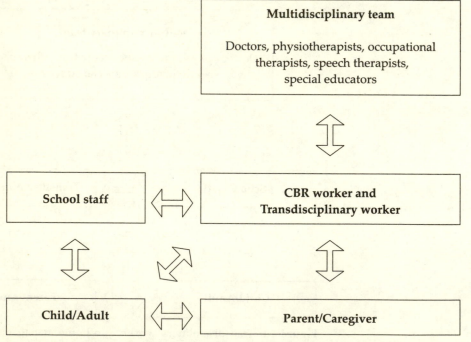

Figure 4.2: Transdisciplinary working in a community based rehabilitation setting

a Transdisciplinary way, and to some extent are capable of assessing, planning and carrying out management programmes, they are not trained to the same level as the Transdisciplinary workers who have undertaken the training as described in Chapter 3. The knowledge of CBR workers will be slightly limited in comparison. Nevertheless, thay have the opportunity to learn from the Transdisciplinary worker during the visits to seek advice and inputs. The Transdisciplinary worker will be able to carry out more detailed and complex assessments and help with planning the input that is required. The child and its family will receive most of their inputs from the CBR worker, but will also have the advantage of seeing the Transdisciplinary worker intermittently.

The relationship to the multidisciplinary team is then similar to the model described earlier; the CBR worker and the Transdisciplinary worker will have a role in liaising with the team and communicating the most relevant information, and of course supporting and reassuring the parents. Again the Transdisciplinary worker will have a large role in liaising with the school that the child attends.

Transdisciplinary working in a day centre setting (see Figure 4.3)

In this setting the class teacher is the Transdisciplinary worker. It is this person who does the assessments and programme planning for each individual child. Here, however, there is likely to be more ready access to the multidisciplinary team, and therefore, there will be more input from them during the assessments, particularly in complex cases and programme planning stages. As in the case of Vidya Sagar, the trainers of the Transdisciplinary course will also be available as mentors to the teachers, to advise on designing integrated programmes for the child in the classroom setting.

The teacher (Transdisciplinary worker in this model) will liaise with all the other departments during the planning stage so that as much of the child's programme as possible, be it in the classroom, creative movement, computer room or wherever, will be Transdisciplinary in nature. For example, it may be possible

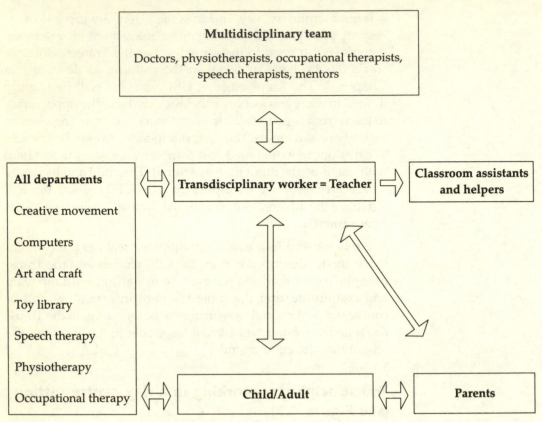

Figure 4.3: Transdisciplinary working in a day centre setting

to work on perceptual problems during gross motor activities in physiotherapy or creative movement, and communication can always be included during any session the child attends inside or outside the classroom. Positioning needs can also be met in any department throughout the school, be it in the speech therapy, art and craft or computers rooms. Where this is not possible, (for example, many gross motor activities are difficult to carry out in the classroom), the child can continue to attend the separate department.

All members of the staff in school, including classroom assistants and ayahs (nursemaid or nanny), should have attended workshops on various elements of therapy so they can work in a Transdisciplinary way as far as possible, even if they have not completed the Transdisciplinary course itself.

Transdisciplinary assessment

The flow diagram (Figure 4.4) shows the process that a Transdiciplinary worker goes through when carrying out an assessment of a child. When one is assessing so many elements of a child's development, it is not possible to have just one assessment. This is why, after taking the initial details of birth history,

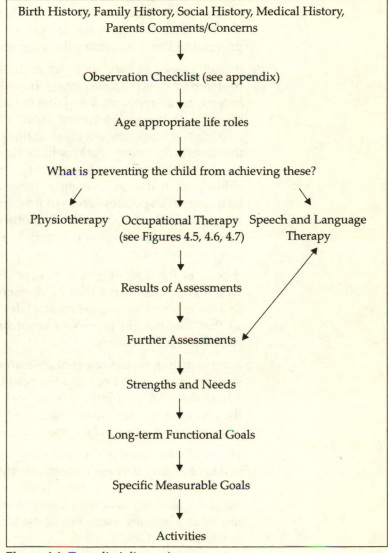

Figure 4.4: Transdisciplinary Assessment

family history, drug history and social history as well as the parents' comments, the next stage is to carry out observations of the child. The Transdisciplinary workers are currently using an observation checklist (see appendix) that was developed for use primarily in the classroom. As they do not always see the child in a classroom setting, the use of this checklist has to be modified accordingly. After looking at the checklist, they consider the expected life roles of that child, and the gaps between what is observed and what would be expected. From these comparisons they then try to consider what factors may be preventing the child from achieving these life roles.

In some cases, it may seem immediately obvious where the problem lies, and in many cases Transdisciplinary workers, or indeed any therapist, may feel that they instinctively know what the main problem is. However, in order to try and prevent overlooking certain significant areas at this point in the assessment, the Transdisciplinary workers have flow diagrams (Figure 4.5, 4.6, 4.7) that have been designed to act as prompts. The idea behind this is that by looking at these diagrams attention can be drawn to all possible areas of problems. Disregarding those where no difficulty is perceived, another area may be picked to investigate first, while the rest may be kept in mind for assessment at a later date.

A copy of the flow diagrams is kept with the child's notes on which the assessments that have been done are highlighted and the areas for investigation at a later date are also indicated, so that the thought processes regarding assessment for this child can easily be seen.

After deciding on the relevant assessments to be done, the assessments are carried out and the results looked at in detail for where the problems inter-link, or influence each other. From the results it is often clear what, if any, further investigations or assessments need to be done.

When all the assessments are completed, the strengths and needs of a child become clearer and the goals can then be set. These goals are set with the involvement of the parents and the child, as much as possible, and relate to the age appropriate life roles. There are examples of the kinds of goals that are set in Chapter 7—Case Studies.

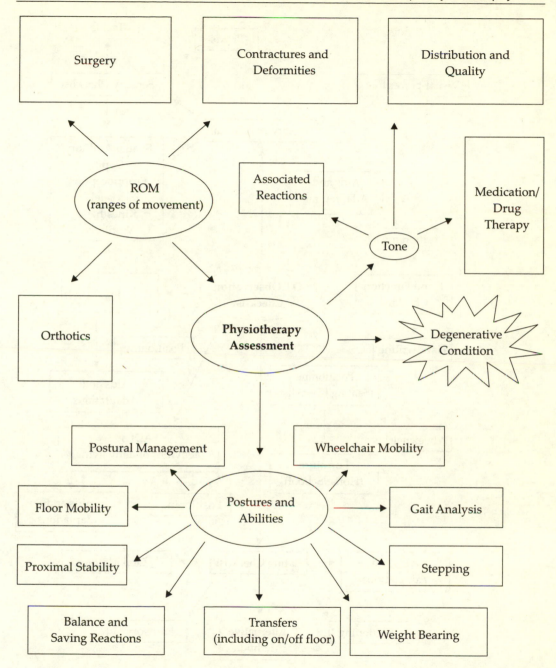

Figure 4.5: Physiotherapy assessment

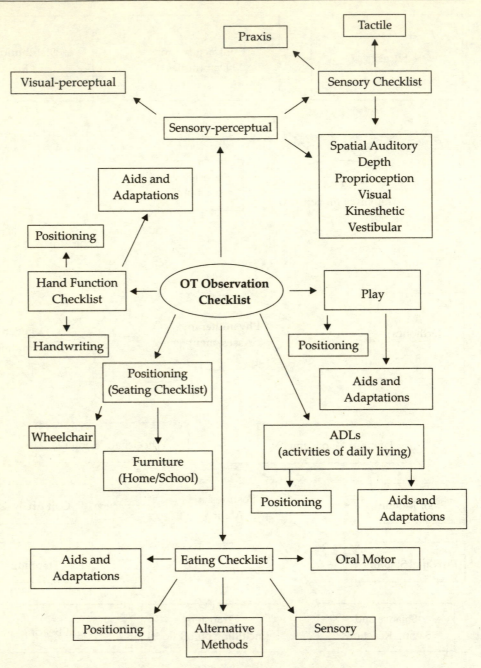

Figure 4.6: OT (occupational therapy) observation checklist

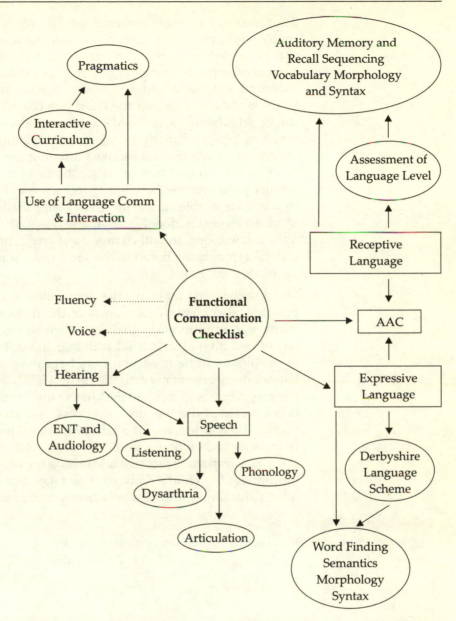

Figure 4.7: Functional communication checklist

The functional goals are broken down into more specific measurable goals, which are the components that make up the skill that is needed to carry out a functional task. To give a very general example, a functional goal may be for the child to dress independently, but in order to achieve this she/he needs to improve her/his balance and the hand function. A specific goals can be set relating to the child's ability to balance for a certain length of time, and another separate goal relating to the ability to carry out a fine motor task like buttoning, for example. As a team we have found that breaking the tasks down into these smaller goals enables the child to feel a sense of achievement, as the team is able to see progress being made towards the ultimate, more functional goals. It also means that the activities a child is working on will change more frequently, preventing the child from being bored of the same tasks being carried out for months on end.

The activities that make up the programme should, as far as possible, also combine elements of the different goals. For example, communication goals can often be incorporated into any other activity that a child is doing, and different postures or positions can be used that may help develop strength or balance during the many activities in the child's day. Integrating the programmes in this manner has many benefits. The child is not aware of the therapy in process, and so compliance is greater. There is less risk of a skill being developed in isolation from other tasks where it could be used. And of course, there is the very important fact that addressing the needs of the child throughout the child's daily routine takes less time and is a more natural way for the whole family to function.

5

The Need for Appropriate Therapy

At the time of writing, six of the nine original core team members are still at Vidya Sagar, though unfortunately three have had to leave the centre due to various family commitments. These six are some of the senior staff at Vidya Sagar and between them they work in four of the departments that Vidya Sagar comprises: home management; out-patients/advisory clinic; day centre; and CBR. All have noted big changes in the way they are able to work after becoming Transdisciplinary workers.

Home management

The home management department has two Transdisciplinary workers, one special educator, two physiotherapists and a speech therapy assistant, who also underwent the speech therapy module of the Transdisciplinary course. The most notable changes that have occurred since the Transdisciplinary training are:

More children being seen by the same number of staff

The children receive less sessions overall, but these sessions constitute an integrated programme, combining education, speech therapy, occupational therapy and physiotherapy. This allows better use of the therapists, who are now able to spend more time with children with specific physiotherapy or speech therapy needs, rather than having to carry out the therapy programmes for all the children attending the department.

> The younger children who need a lot of movement therapy and the initial concepts of education, play, etc., can be best handled by the physiotherapists. Also the therapists have more time to spend with children with specific therapy needs.
>
> — Sadiya

Holistic intervention, a reality

Although only two of the staff are Transdisciplinary workers, the whole department is functioning in a more holistic way. Assessments are done by the whole team and goals set according to the life roles. Setting goals relating to life roles is more relevant for the children and their families. The individual professionals then work with the children but in a holistic way as far as possible.

> Assessments, I am able to do them without thinking. I realise automatically what assessments I need to do. I can now plan goals relating to the child's life roles, and therefore all areas are covered immediately.... I feel it is much more holistic. I think we were previously underestimating certain children and I think the kids can do a lot more now.
>
> — Sadiya

Prioritisation of a child's needs

This is closely linked to the two statements earlier; with better assessments and more relevant goal setting it is easier to prioritise a child's needs. This in turn leads to more efficient and effective use of staff in the department.

Better support to parents

With the level of knowledge the Transdisciplinary workers now have, they are more confident in explaining to parents their child's condition, the relevance of certain therapies and how to carry out the child's management programme during the daily routine.

But of course, parents did not immediately accept the changes in the way children were managed in the department:

> Initially they didn't like it, cutting down on sessions, they felt they were getting ignored a bit, they didn't think we could do everything in one session. One parent kept asking for all three sessions but I have worked with her help her to understand the needs of her child, so she is more comfortable now.
>
> – Sadiya

Out-patients/advisory clinic

Lakshmi, the main person in out-patients clinic, is from the original core team. Other staff from the school also do sessions once or twice a week. The changes that have occurred since the Transdisciplinary training are similar to those in home management, with a few additions.

Better time management

As Lakshmi no longer has to wait for therapists to come and assess a child, being able to carry out all assessments herself, less time is spent in waiting. Although some of the other staff that also work in out-patients have not undergone the Transdisciplinary training as yet, this is not a problem. Lakshmi allocates children to them with needs relevant to that member of staff's area of expertise and is usually around in the department to help out with other areas as needed.

Integrated programmes

As with home management, the goals and programmes are related to life roles, and so are more holistic in nature. Lakshmi feels that this approach has helped to give parents a better understanding of the needs of their child, and thus increased their motivation.

> The parents say things like 'it is the first time we have understood about our child, we never knew she/he could do all this.' We very often get families who have had advice or input only in therapy. This is usually along the lines of passive movements. So they often seem a lot more motivated after a session with us when we have taught them how to facilitate their child to move.
>
> – Lakshmi

Inclusion

With the change in understanding about their children, parents are gradually coming to accept that their children do not necessarily need to attend a special school.

> We have a large number on the waiting list; everyone wants admission into the day centre, but we are trying to explain that it is just not necessary for all children. We are gradually getting more of them to accept integration into mainstream schools.
>
> – Lakshmi

Better communication with doctors

Since undertaking the Transdisciplinary training a closer relationship with the medical team has been formed. More children are being referred for bo-tox or surgery, with joint assessments of the children being done with the doctors. Before the Transdisciplinary training, some children from the day centre were chosen for bo-tox therapy but the outcome was not successful. Now in close liaison with the doctors better choices are made and the correct follow up therapy is ensured. So far results have been good with high child and parent satisfaction.

> A big difference for me is communicating with the doctors. I can understand the terminology now and feel more confident discussing things with them. Last time we tried Bo-tox (before Transdisciplinary training), we had no idea of what to expect or what to do, except what we had read in the pamphlet. Now it is much clearer. I am able to judge whether a child is OK for bo-tox or not. We have found that the kids who have had bo-tox and had follow up therapy here also have done really well, maintaining the goals we

set for the bo-tox intervention many months later. The parents have given very positive feedback also—I think that is because we could explain clearly what we were aiming for and what they could expect.

—Lakshmi

Day centre

Sudha, core team member is the head of the day centre and has been able to influence the running of the day centre in a number of ways since her Transdisciplinary training.

Prioritisation

Being able to carry out assessments more easily and appropriately, and to set goals relating to life roles, Sudha is better equipped to advise on how a child's time must be spent. Rather than everyone spending an equal amount of time in the therapy room, for example three sessions a week, the aims of the child are considered more carefully. For example, a child may have potential to develop his/her communication skills, but only limited potential to develop independent movement and mobility. For such a child it may be more appropriate to have more sessions in the computer room looking at access to education and communication, with the child's therapy needs being met mainly through postural management and group therapy.

This type of change has allowed for better use of the therapy staff, with more staff being available to handle some of those heavier or more complex cases that need two people to carry out a therapy programme.

Of course, the main benefit of this change is that the children's needs are being addressed more appropriately, with more successes being evident and more motivation and increased self-esteem observed in the children.

It has made a difference in therapy where we now realise if a child needs two therapists, or less frequent therapy times. We also look at sensory perceptual aspects in the therapy room, so the activities they are doing are different. We see changes more quickly and they move on to new activities rather than staying on the same thing for months.

— Sudha

Advice to teachers and other staff

As head of the day centre, Sudha has always been inclined to give advice or suggestions when she felt something should be done differently, but now she is more sure of what she is saying and why changes should be made.

> I was always making suggestions, I didn't just start now, but now I am sure about what I am saying. I am not so vague now. If you are vague, no one will take you seriously. I used to get into a lot of arguments with therapists, but now I can argue my point better and they respect that. Having so much knowledge has improved the quality of the therapy I do.
>
> – Sudha

Communication with doctors

Sudha, like Lakshmi, has also worked with the doctors as more children have been referred for surgery or bo-tox. She has found that since her understanding of technical jargon and terminology has increased, she is able to communicate more confidently.

> We are speaking the same language now which really helps. Before you wouldn't know what something was in technical terms, but would try so hard to explain to them (doctors), but they wouldn't understand what you were getting at ... they would brush you aside thinking you don't know anything. Now with doctors you can make suggestions and it does make a difference. You can give so much more detail about some areas of a child that they don't know which will affect the outcome of their inputs.
>
> – Sudha

Community based rehabilitation (CBR)

Mallika from the core team is responsible for co-coordinating with all the CBR partners, and also running the training programmes for the CBR workers. She feels the Transdisciplinary training has greatly helped her to carry out her work.

Maintaining numbers of CBR projects that Vidya Sagar is able to work with

An important point here is that over the past few years quite a few of the more senior staff and therapists who used to be involved in CBR visits are no longer able to travel to the rural communities due to personal reasons, family commitments, etc. This would have significantly affected the ability of the teams going out on a regular basis from Vidya Sagar, if it were not for the Transdisciplinary workers. However, since the Transdisciplinary training, individual Transdisciplinary workers are able to answer most queries they encounter on a CBR visit, and therefore partnerships with rural projects have been maintained, even with less staff being available.

> Many of the senior staff have moved on over the past couple of years, but since the training I don't need to rely on individual professionals so much. A lot of staff involved in CBR teams have gone and if we hadn't had the Transdisciplinary training we wouldn't have been able to continue working with so many projects. We are doing the same number of projects and we can say we haven't had to compromise on the quality. The people who go on CBR are equipped to look at all aspects of the child.
>
> — Mallika

More holistic training of CBR workers

CBR workers come to Vidya Sagar once a year for training, either for an introductory course lasting six to ten days, or a refresher/ advanced course for approximately five days. Even before the core team did their Transdisciplinary training, the CBR workers were Transdisciplinary workers in a relative sense. They were receiving training in speech, education, physiotherapy and occupational therapy, from the individual professionals at Vidya Sagar, but at a less technical level than what the core team has now received.

These training courses would take a lot of planning and organisation in order to coordinate based on the availability of different professionals. Since the Transdisciplinary training of the core team, Mallika has found she is less reliant on the input of the individual therapists, with members of the core team being able to carry out the majority of the training programmes. This has helped Mallika when staff numbers have reduced.

Also, planning the course has become easier. Mallika is able to plan a holistic programme, starting with the concept of life roles, and how to facilitate this, instead of looking at all the therapies individually.

It has made me a lot more confident. We are training a lot more people. It has helped me to plan a training programme, looking at all areas. I know what is required, not that I know everything, but I know what the gaps are and what other help I need. We don't always need to give very specialist skills to CBR workers and so the core team are able to handle teaching that level of knowledge. We can simplify terminology.

– Mallika

Confidence on field visits

The greater level of knowledge in all areas of therapy has obviously helped enormously on field visits, but it hasn't stopped the team from knowing their limitations.

Confidence on field visits is also a lot more, even if I don't immediately have an answer, I can visualise the child, take relevant information and go back to a professional for more advice.

– Mallika

And from the first batch of trainees

On the first Transdisciplinary course that was run there were four teachers from the staff at Vidya Sagar; two of them are also mothers of children with special needs. All four of them have comments to make on the changes the course has made to their lives, both professional and personal.

Teachers at the day centre

Assessments

In addition to being able to carry out the assessments more easily, the staff are finding that, as they now understand the results and implications more clearly, they are better able to think of relevant activities for the children to do within the classroom.

As the other departments have already noted, goal setting has become easier with more appropriate priorities being realised for the children.

It has helped me a lot in goal setting and planning activities for kids. When I have assessment results I can plan and apply what I have found out.

– Madhy

Activities within the classroom

Since the training, the teachers have been more aware of carrying out therapy aspects of the children's programmes within the classroom, understanding the necessity for incorporating all areas of the child's capabilities or physical needs as far as possible, for example, postural changes, or use of a communication chart.

> Like with Sridhar, we are trying to do all activities with him using his chart so everyone now interacts with him more.
>
> – Madhy

Communication with other members of the team

Increased comprehension of technical terms has helped the teaching staff to express their concerns, understand problems and deal with them effectively through clearer communication with the other members of the medical team.

Parents

Radha is the mother of Sunderam and Sriram, seventeen-year-old twin boys, who have cerebral palsy. She also teaches at Vidya Sagar within the home management department. Meenakshi is the music teacher at Vidya Sagar and has a nine-year-old son, Kedar, with cerebral palsy, who attends mainstream school.

Time management

Both parents found that their time management has improved since the training course, the most important issue being that they do not feel guilty about not allocating separate therapy time for the children every day. This helps in all sorts of ways, allowing more family time, less tension in the family and, very importantly, a better rapport with the children.

> Now I am able to save a lot of time. They are becoming more and more independent because of the adaptations I have put—where I was giving them physical prompts before I am now only giving them verbal prompts, so I can be in another room. They are gradually learning the sequence of movements that they need to do to perform a task, so their motor planning is improved and this again helps their independence. This gives them motivation to do it and

They don't always realise they're doing therapy.

their self-esteem has gone up like anything. Now they are able to say to others how they do something, so how the other people need to help them. They know how to ask for help. They are much happier now that they don't realise when they are doing therapy, which is helping me to build a good rapport with them. My husband is also happy, he understands that they don't need to do separate therapy but that they are doing their therapy through functional tasks.

– Radha

Kedar was bored with therapy, but now he's happy. He doesn't know when he is doing therapy. I find more time for myself now in the evening. Earlier I would feel depressed when I didn't have time to relax, but now I am happy. The whole family is happier because in the evenings we have time to spend together.

– Meenakshi

Less dependence on professionals

Radha has particularly noticed that she is less dependent on the therapists now, she is confident to make adaptations in her home to help her sons develop their independence. Understanding their needs better, by looking at life roles, has also helped her prioritise what is needed and what is appropriate for them.

In therapy I needed help with everything, right from positioning. I was not confident that what I was doing with my children was right or wrong and at home there is no-one to correct you. I always had to call the therapist home to check if adaptations were correct. Now I know what I was doing wrong and am correcting things. I am also able to make changes at home, adaptations, etc., exactly what the children need.

– Radha

Understanding their children better

The increase in knowledge has led both parents to understand their children better. For example, where previously they thought the main problem was due to motor difficulties, they now real-ise that sensory problems are also a significant factor in their child's inability to do something. Meenakshi has found that since she understands Kedar's speech problems more clearly now, she is carrying out more relevant activities with him.

Parents understand their child's needs better.

Understanding their options better

Another very significant point for these parents is that the knowledge they have gained has helped them make informed choices about additional therapy input for their children.

> With therapy we used to run from pillar to post without knowing what it was, or if it would really benefit Kedar, but now I will read the details and think, using my knowledge, and decide whether it will be useful for Kedar.
>
> — Meenakshi

Besides, not being intimidated by the medical terminology that doctors use has helped the parents understand what medical professionals are suggesting.

> Although I am not actually questioning doctors, I know how to take things in the right way, I don't get intimidated. Like if a doctor says 'He needs surgery', two years ago I was scared, but now I am not scared. I know what he wants to do and why, what exactly they will do to help balance, correct posture, etc. I can ask questions—not foolish ones anymore. I can talk to them with confidence.
>
> — Radha

These are comments made by parents of children with cerebral palsy who have done the Transdisciplinary training course. The following chapter will be looking in more detail at comments from parents of children who are being managed by a Transdisciplinary worker.

Comments from core-team members who have since left

Lavanya

Lavanya is a physiotherapist who did her B.Sc. in physiotherapy in Chennai and then a special education diploma at Vidya Sagar. She was working at Vidya Sagar as a physiotherapist and special educator when the first Action Health Trainer arrived. She was keen to undertake the Transdisciplinary training and was a valuable member of the team. Unfortunately for Vidya Sagar, she left to study for her Masters degree in Melbourne, Australia, before the occupational therapy and speech therapy sections of the training were completed.

However, she was very keen to give her comments on the training she did receive as she gained much knowledge from it.

> Paediatrics was one area that was not given adequate importance in my undergraduate physiotherapy course. As an undergraduate student I had observed some physiotherapists doing only passive range of movement exercises and occasionally some muscle strengthening, similar to that done for a patient with a musculoskeletal condition. Also, physiotherapists were applying the same principles and techniques to treat adults and children with disabilities. So when I attended the physiotherapy training at Vidya Sagar I was a physiotherapist who didn't have any structured formal training in paediatric physiotherapy. Since this was my area of interest I had gained knowledge from textbooks that were available at my college. Most of my experience in handling and treating children with disabilities had come mainly from the special education course at Vidya Sagar and also from my work at Vidya Sagar as physiotherapist and special educator. This programme remarkably increased my levels of confidence in managing children with cerebral palsy with varied presentations. It sharpened and added to my handling skills. The programme also taught me how to set SMART (Specific, Measurable, Achievable, Relevant, Time bound) goals appropriate to the child's functional capabilities taking into consideration the child's and the family's needs.
>
> – Lavanya

Lavanya now works as a paediatric physiotherapist in an acute care hospital (National University Hospital, Singapore) and sees children with cerebral palsy as out-patients. She is also attached to a child development clinic in the community and feels that the skills she learnt from the Vidya Sagar course definitely help her manage the children she currently sees.

She suggests that there should be more input on sensory integration and task-orientated approaches on the course offered at Vidya Sagar. Both these elements were covered by the occupational therapist who did the training with the core team and are part of the integrated Transdisciplinary course now offered by Vidya Sagar.

Lavanya's comments echo Poonam's comments in Chapter 1, where she describes how physiotherapists would come to work at Vidya Sagar with very little training in paediatrics. Vidya Sagar does take students from physiotherapy colleges for a two-week period to expose them to children with different disabilities. Unfortunately, they come in quite large groups and there is often mixed degrees of interest within these groups. Occasionally, some students do not seem particularly receptive to being taught physiotherapy from a non-physiotherapist (e.g., Transdisciplinary worker) despite the years of experience that the person may have had.

Meenakshi

Meenakshi was the principal of the day centre during the Transdisciplinary training course. She undertook the training in all three areas of therapy, but left Vidya Sagar shortly after due to family reasons. She now works in Oman at a school for children with autism.

When commenting on her thoughts on the course in general, Meenakshi reflected that prior to the training, lack of confidence in her abilities in the therapy areas had cost her and her students' time.

> Prior to the course, as a class teacher I had lots of queries about the therapy programmes of my students—speech, occupational therapy and physiotherapy. Even though I felt intuitively I could answer the questions I had, I didn't have the confidence to implement them. I would always wait for the therapy departments to give me the go-ahead before doing anything, which invariably took time. And by the time they came with the answer I would always have new questions.
>
> – Meenakshi

Despite the fact that she no longer works with children with cerebral palsy, Meenakshi feels that the training has benefited her in the work she is currently doing. She particularly finds the approach to goal setting useful.

> Initially my goals read: 1. Reading; 2. Writing; 3. Maths; etc. Now when I set goals I look at all four aspects: education, physiotherapy,

occupational therapy and speech/communication aspects. I also make sure that the goals look into all the three areas of life roles, work, leisure and self-maintenance. I think I did do this unconsciously before but now it has become more systematic and therefore gets done more definitely. The occupational therapy inputs and speech and language inputs I received are of immense help in my work now. I also use the physio inputs in improving the overall physical development of the children, especially gait patterns. I feel more confident and am able to articulate and write it down while I am setting goals for them.

– Meenakshi

Regarding thoughts on ways to improve the course, Meenakshi mentions the importance of practical experience in developing confidence, and that, if possible, this element should be increased in the course. She also mentions that working in her current job she has received more training in speech and communication, namely, Applied Behavioural Analysis methods, which are aimed at improving articulation. She recommends that these aspects be included in the Transdisciplinary training course as the techniques would be appropriate for those children with cerebral palsy who have problems of dyspraxia.

Anuradha (Anu)

Anu was head of home management and also coordinator for the CBR projects when the Action Health–Skillshare partnership began. She had worked at Vidya Sagar for several years and had previous experience in women's issues and community health. She had worked closely with Poonam when discussing the need to develop a Transdisciplinary worker and was involved in the planning of the project from the beginning.

She undertook the physiotherapy training and the majority of the occupational therapy along with speech and language elements. After leaving Vidya Sagar she has been working at an organisation in Delhi that decides on funding for NGO projects. On a recent visit to Chennai she gave her comments on the Transdisciplinary concept and its relevance throughout the country from the new perspective her job has given her.

One of the most important points that she raised was that the government is keen to fund and support projects where the village communities are being empowered to help themselves. Coming from a background of working with people with disabilities Anu recognises the fact that although obviously empowerment is an excellent underlying goal, there are many people in village communities with disabilities who will still be excluded from these projects. There needs to be someone with specialised knowledge in management of disability to facilitate these people and their families to access the empowerment projects.

> In rural projects like the ones that Vidya Sagar is involved with, cerebral palsy is one of the main conditions being addressed. In other areas there are not so many people with knowledge of how to treat cerebral palsy; they are generally working with more development issues and attitudes. If a person with a disability requires technical inputs, then this kind of Transdisciplinary worker would be useful, particularly at a grassroots level—as many people as possible, so that workers on these development projects are able to address the needs of people with multiple disabilities.
>
> — Anu

The next important point was regarding cost. The funding organisation that Anu is employed with is keen that the majority of funding allocated to a project goes directly to the individuals that the project is working with. This again would support the development of a Transdisciplinary worker.

> I think this kind of worker would be very useful in rural projects, as a multidisciplinary team would definitely not be available. Health services in these rural areas are not able to employ a full multidisciplinary team. Cost is obviously an important issue. If you are looking at a multidisciplinary team there will be a lot of funds going on salary, not directly to the recipients of the service. The government is looking at funding projects where more of the funds go directly to the poor. In these cases the Transdisciplinary worker is relevant. If five lakh is given to a project and four lakh is spent on salaries, a lot less of the village people will benefit because not all of them will need all the services provided by the multidisciplinary team or whoever. So a Transdisciplinary worker would make a lot more sense. Working with the CBR worker, increasing awareness, educating people and increasing the working capacities of people with disabilities, they could also train other workers

like teachers and traditional birth attendants. They could develop a referral service to somewhere like Vidya Sagar for example, or to a multidisciplinary team, but the Transdisciplinary worker could be directly in the field.

– Anu

The other area where Anu feels the development of this concept is particularly important is in the area of inclusion. With her own experience of having a colleague with a hearing impairment in the office where she worked, Anu realised how important it is for everyone involved in the inclusion process to be adequately trained.

It would also work with professionals who need to broaden their skills, otherwise some of these ideas they have are just a set of words, just something from a discussion, for example, wanting to develop the concept of inclusions. It is not enough to just have someone on your team to say that inclusion is happening. For example, when I was working with someone with a hearing impairment, we needed to be taught how to interact together, mime was not enough. He had to learn to write things down and we also had to learn some sign language. So professionals need to know how to broaden their skills to make a concept like inclusion really work. We cannot do it with our narrow areas of specialisation.

– Anu

Still on the point of inclusion, Anu felt it important to stress how inclusions should not be mere statistics, but it should be ensured that children with disabilities benefit from it by gaining entry into mainstream schools. Again, as mentioned earlier, we at Vidya Sagar believe that the concept of a Transdisciplinary worker is particularly relevant in the context of inclusive education, with one professional being able to address all the child's needs and answer all the class teacher's queries, thus facilitating a smooth process of inclusion in mainstream schools.

Transdisciplinary workers and inclusion will be discussed further in Chapter 9—Reflections and Recommendations.

6 Enriching the Quality of Life

It was important for the staff involved in the complete process of developing and implementing Transdisciplinary working to find out whether the parents had actually felt a change in the service provided and to hear their reactions. The decision was taken to interview parents directly rather than use a questionnaire. There were two reasons for this. One was that the lack of command over language and the low level of academic education could affect their ability to express themselves while responding to the questionnaire. The second reason was that we wanted to try and encourage the parents to speak freely about their experiences of the care given to their child at Vidya Sagar. A range of questions were agreed upon to use as a basis to generate a discussion with the parents, but the questions were to act more as a guide, with plenty of opportunity for the parents to take the conversation where they wanted.

It was unlikely that parents would feel confident of openly critisising the services of Vidya Sagar when talking to a staff member. We, therefore, facilitated constructive criticism from the parents so that they would have an opportunity to share if they felt that some needs of the child were not being addressed.

The questions that were asked broadly covered the following areas:

Previous experiences
What inputs had they had before coming to Vidya Sagar?

What had they liked/disliked about this input?

Why had they come to Vidya Sagar?

Awareness of the Transdisciplinary approach

Were they aware of a different approach being used at the centre, with one person being responsible for their child's care?

If they had been at the Centre prior to this change in approach, what changes had they noticed?

Management of their child

Had the change in management affected them, their child and the whole family?

What were their feelings on the programme that they were following for their child?

Their child

Had there been a change in the child's attitude to therapy?

Have the children and parents been involved in setting the goals of treatment?

Is progress being made?

Has the change in input altered the way in which the child is included in family life?

Overall

Do they feel that they are getting enough input and information with this approach?

What have been the reactions of the family to the change in the approach?

Do they still wish to try other approaches of management?

Any other comments?

The parents interviewed were primarily from the home management department at Vidya Sagar as this is where the change in approach is most comprehensively implemented. Within the day centre the change is taking place more slowly as members of the staff are gradually being trained. Within the home management department there are three members of the staff who have undergone the Transdisciplinary training and so the whole department is functioning differently, with one person being responsible for all areas of the child's programme.

Introducing the parents

Jayalakshmi

Jayalakshmi is the mother of Hari, an eight-year-old boy, who suffers from frequent seizures and is hypotonic. She is a science graduate who left her job in a transport company to take care of Hari. She did a beautician's course but later decided to do her diploma in special education.

Hari has been attending Vidya Sagar with his mother for four years, and the staff report that Jayalakshmi is a very empowered woman, and frequently undertakes training of the other mothers.

A year or so prior to arriving at Vidya Sagar, Jayalakshmi had taken her son to another centre, where she attended their programme

We have more time to spend as a family.

only for a month. This was partly because she was working at that time and was unable to attend frequently, but also because she was unhappy with the way that the staff treated the parents and the children.

She states that before coming to Vidya Sagar she did not really understand her son.

> I didn't really understand about Hari before I came here. Before, we were going for therapy near our house, they would just move his joints and keep them loose, but since I came here I realised how I could handle him to encourage him.
>
> – Jayalakshmi

She seems quite happy that there is just one person handling Hari's whole programme and understands that therapy is being done alongside education. The most important change noted by her since coming to Vidya Sagar is her increased confidence in what she is doing for her son.

> The family used to ask 'you are going to school daily now—is he able to walk yet?' They still don't fully understand Hari's condition, but I am confident to explain what I am doing and why. I know Hari is improving. I still feel guilty if I relax, I feel I should be spending time with Hari, but I do think I am more relaxed while doing his therapy—I sing! He also likes learning and therapy now, he likes me to read aloud to him, whatever I am reading.
>
> – Jayalakshmi

When asked if she felt she would like to try other management approaches for Hari, Jayalakshmi had a clear and term response.

> I know about my child, I know what to expect from him. I won't believe someone if they say 'take him there—he will walk within a week.'
>
> – Jayalakshmi

P. Vasugi

Vasugi is the mother of Arvind Raj, a six-year-old boy with multiple disabilities. She and her husband moved to Chennai from the Andaman Islands (a Union Territory of India) to get input for Arvind Raj at Vidya Sagar. They initially intended to stay one year but have already been here for two and may try to extend their stay. Vasugi is a B.Ed. (Bachelor of Education) graduate and her husband Rajkumar is a junior engineer in Andaman Lakshwadeep Harbour Works. He has a diploma in Civil Engineering and they live in the quarters allotted by the company. Vasugi has left her employment and stays at home to support Arvind Raj.

When Vasugi first came to the Centre she was suffering from depression and stomach ulcers caused by it. She found it difficult to eat and only visited the Centre only once a week. She no longer has health problems (no actual treatment has been given) and attends home management three times a week with her son.

Prior to Vidya Sagar, the family had tried to get input for Arvind Raj and had received a splint for his leg and some physiotherapy. The programme was only once a year and little advice other than the physiotherapy was offered.

Since coming to Vidya Sagar there have been inputs in all areas of Arvind Raj's development, education, communication, self-help skills, and Vasugi has learned about facilitating correct patterns of movement. Vasugi still felt that physiotherapy was a priority for Arvind Raj, though at Vidya Sagar he has undergone bo-tox injections and surgery, both of which have markedly improved his motor abilities.

These improvements have in turn enhanced his ability to take part in activities of daily living, and Vasugi is gradually coming to understand the importance of the other areas of development.

Vasugi appreciates the support from other parents and the staff and is keen to continue receiving more input. The family now hopes to stay another year in Chennai.

Renuka

Renuka and M.K. Thiruvenkatasamy are the parents of Rajashree, a six-year-old girl. They are both B. Com. (Bachelor of Commerce) graduates with Thiruvenkatasamy having done ICWA (Institute of Cost and Works Accountants) and now working as an accounts manager. They belong to the middle income group and live in a joint family with thirteen members. Renuka and her daughter had been coming to the out-patients clinic at Vidya Sagar for six months before transferring to the home management programme four months ago.

Renuka had tried a couple of other places where the input for Rajashree had always been divided between different therapists. Previously she had experienced working in a group with everyone getting the same input. She had found these inputs less specific to Rajashree. Renuka finds her experience at Vidya Sagar quite different.

> Here I am gaining more information regarding the child's welfare in all aspects. I know more about my child now, what her needs are and how to help her. She has a communication chart now. I had one before but I didn't know how to use it properly. I can give her choices now.

Renuka also spoke about how she found that her needs were listened to by the staff, and taken into consideration when goals for the programme were being set. She is another parent who feels to have benefited a lot from the support she has received from both staff and other parents at Vidya Sagar.

> I am keen to give support to others, I have suffered a lot and I feel I can now help others.
>
> — Renuka

Fazila

Fazila is the mother of Raqeeb, an 11-year-old boy whose case study is included in Chapter 7. He has mental retardation as a result of a metabolic disorder and has been attending Vidya Sagar's home management department for two years.

Fazila had tried various other places and had received some inputs on play and therapy for Raqeeb. At a time when she was feeling depressed she met another parent who recommended that she try Vidya Sagar. And, she has not regretted her decision.

> I am getting inputs in all areas, all working towards independence. Now he is able to focus on people much better and his social participation has improved, so has his cooperation. I am more relaxed, but still don't seem to have any more spare time—I would rather be doing things with Raqeeb.

Fazila, like many of the other mothers, commended the support she received from everyone at the Centre.

> I feel I am getting input from everyone here, everyone is interested in his progress. All the staff and parents will help me out. I am convinced that what is being done here is for the best.

Sridevi

Sridevi is the mother of Ramakrishna, a nine-year-old boy with mental retardation. They have been attending Vidya Sagar for six years. Sridevi has education to the level of SSLC (Secondary School Leaving Certificate), as has her husband who is a police constable. They live in a joint family of nine people.

Sridevi is very clear about what she is receiving from the staff at Vidya Sagar.

> I am getting inputs for my son in all areas, education, self-help skills, physiotherapy and speech therapy. My son has developed a lot of independence since coming here, his manipulative skills have improved and he does a lot of ADLs by himself. Working with Radha, it is easy to follow the routine in the house.
>
> —Sridevi

She is also pleased that all the family members have noticed improvements, and she herself now finds time to relax and even watch television in the afternoon. She has no desire to go elsewhere but is keen for more input from Vidya Sagar.

Sheila

Sheila is the mother of D'John, also known as Sarosh. He is 12 years old and has multiple disabilities following encephalitis at the age of five years. They have been coming to Vidya Sagar for ten months.

Sheila had tried another centre for input about four years ago, but did not like the way her child was handled. When told about Vidya Sagar by a friend, Sheila could not accept or imagine her son attending a centre for children with disabilities as he had, prior to his illness, been going to a normal school. She had tried some drug therapy at a hospital but felt that the side effects were making Sarosh's overall condition worse.

When she did eventually come to Vidya Sagar she felt she had made the right decision.

> I like the way they handle the child here and also the way they support the parent. I am very much changed now. I am ready to face anything for my child. I can face my family members. I can tell them what the problems are and how to handle them. There is a lot of support here, helping us deal with the problems we are facing. I am very confident now. I want even more confidence!
>
> — Sheila

In addition to the increase in the level of her confidence Sheila has noticed a marked change in her son's attitude.

> Sarosh is much calmer now, especially in public places. I feel very satisfied that my son is getting something useful. Earlier, I used to spend so much time thinking 'how can I bring up this child?' but now I am confident. Before, he used to say he could not do something because his hands didn't work properly, but now with help he can achieve so much. He is finding the difference. He didn't want to try before, but now he does. He is much more cooperative. Now I know how to teach him and so he is succeeding.
>
> — Sheila

Radha is the staff member responsible for Sarosh's management, and Sheila finds her advice and encouragement very motivating.

> I get so much support from the staff here, like Radha. I thought to myself, she has got two children with disabilities, and if she can do it so can I! She listens to me when I tell her what is important to me, and I feel confident to come and ask if I have any problems.
>
> — Sheila

Sheila is now able to visualise a future for Sarosh.

> I want to give him a good future and make sure he is not too dependent on others. I think the inputs here will help me achieve this for him.
>
> — Sheila

Vidya

Vidya is the mother of Arvindan, an eight-year-old boy and has been coming to Vidya Sagar for one-and-a-half years. Vidya is a post-graduate in Tamil and has plans to study further. Her husband, Manohar, after relocating to Chennai for Arvindan's education, has taken up photography as his profession, although he is a graduate in history. They live as a nuclear family in an independent house.

Though they had not been to any centre for input before coming to Vidya Sagar, Vidya already feels confident in handling her child. She finds that the programme easily fits into her daily routine and the staff are considering her needs. By working towards greater independence for Arvindan she is finding more time for herself.

When asked if she thinks she would like to try other types of management for her son, Vidya replied that she would have to ask the staff at Vidya Sagar for their advice before she tried anything new.

Uma

Uma is the mother of Kamya, a five-year-old girl with athetoid cerebral palsy. They have been coming to Vidya Sagar for three years.

Uma had been to various care centres before coming to Vidya Sagar, but did not find them too helpful. She recalls that in the beginning she did not really understand Kamya's problem and felt that the staff did not understand it either. Kamya was receiving physiotherapy at home when Uma saw an article about Vidya Sagar in the newspaper.

When Uma first came to Vidya Sagar she told Poonam that Kamya did not need therapy as she was already receiving that at home; but Uma soon changed her mind.

> What they do at Vidya Sagar is total therapy. It includes everything, not just moving your arms and legs. I feel my way of handling her is more meaningful now. I don't have therapy time, but everything I do with her is towards meeting her needs. The programme

fits into my routine. It suits Kamya, who is very sensitive to being touched and used to hate therapy. She is more cooperative now.

— Uma

Uma is yet another parent who feels strongly that she has benefited greatly from the support she has received from other parents and the staff at Vidya Sagar.

I have learnt to accept the label of Kamya's condition. I keep reading to find out about it. It is hard for a parent to accept a label for their child. In the first few months at Vidya Sagar it was learning for me, the parent, then I have transferred what I have learnt to my child.

— Uma

It is heartening to learn that Uma and her family have noticed remarkable changes in Kamya since attending Vidya Sagar.

My child started to respond only after coming here. All the family have noticed an improvement in all aspects like communication and movement. She didn't move before she came here. I just regret not coming sooner. I somehow thought a child needed to be three to start school. I feel that I wasted time.

— Uma

As in the case of many other parents, Uma still does not find much time for herself. But she feels more relaxed about leaving Kamya for a few minutes while she goes to another room and does not worry about it any more. Kamya is not calling out for help every five minutes.

Uma's key concern now centres on the future of Kamya. Realising that Kamya will always be dependent on others for at least some of her needs, Uma is concerned about what will happen when she is not able to take care of Kamya. This is one thing Uma would like to have reassurance about in some way.

Conclusions

As explained at the beginning of this chapter, when carrying out the interviews with the parents, we facilitated the discussions with the parents in such a way that they were not influenced by us but felt free to say what they wished to. It was observed that in the interviews the respondents had not really commented on the concept of Transdisciplinary workers as opposed to individual therapists. But after reading the transcripts several times and reflecting on them it became evident that the fact that they did not dwell on the issue was in itself significant.

None of the parents expressed any concern that their child was not receiving individual therapy sessions; instead, all the parents interviewed, without exception, talked more about the overall care their child was receiving. This is a significant change from the routine, as health professionals may observe. All too often parents come to therapy assessments and treatment sessions asking repeatedly when their child will walk. Such unrealistic expectations arise from the fact that the parents do not understand all the issues involving their child's condition. The parents interviewed, all directly or indirectly expressed an understanding of the complexity of their child's needs and holistic care and talked about developing their child's independence without referring directly to compartmentalised outcomes.

A sentiment very clearly shared by all mothers interviewed was the support they received from each other and the staff at Vidya Sagar. While it is not just Transdisciplinary workers who are providing this support, one of the key aims of the concept of Transdisciplinary working is that parents build a good relationship with a single specialist who could provide holistic support. It is envisaged that this individual would answer the queries of concerned parents/families and reduce the frustration and stress that could arise from dealing with a multidisciplinary team. An issue described by Poonam in her experiences as a parent in Chapter 1.

Empowerment of parents is important when working with these families and is something that Vidya Sagar works hard to achieve. The staff in home management carry out parent training workshops, and parents who are confident take part in training the other parents. The Transdisciplinary workers are able to use these sessions to focus on issues like incorporating therapy within the daily routine as much as possible. Sheila, one of the parents, had this to say about the experience:

I have learnt so much from these workshops! I tell the other parents—'You MUST attend these workshops! They are teaching us how to handle our children throughout the day.'

— Sheila

The responses from the parents are clear testimonies that the services provided by the staff at Vidya Sagar have indeed made a difference. Revisiting the underlying beliefs about the management of children with disabilities, outlined in Chapter 1, reiterates that many of these have been achieved, as shared by the parents.

7

Children with Disability Can Be Independent: Case Studies

The following are case studies of some of the children that the core team and the first batch of trainees have worked with both during and since their Transdisciplinary training. I have tried to include as much diversity in terms of clinical presentation of the child, age range and family background in order to illustrate how the Transdisciplinary approach enables the Transdisciplinary worker to address a number of different issues in a holistic manner.

The activities listed are just some examples of those included in the child's programme. Specific details of how each activity fitted into the daily routine has not been given.

Shebagaselvi (Selvi)

Selvi was seven years old when she first came to Vidya Sagar. She had global developmental delay. There was no specific diagnosis reported by her parents and no medical background given except that there had been no birth cry. The only input that she had received so far was in the form of medication, which had not brought about any significant changes to her physical abilities.

Selvi lives in a joint family which is quite well off and has a younger brother who has no health problems.

Initial presentation

Selvi was very irritable, agitated and crying most of the time when she first visited Vidya Sagar. She was

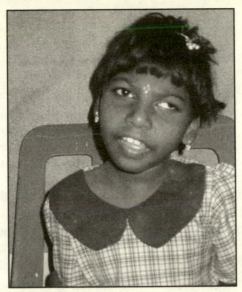

Selvi responds to her name.

totally dependent for all areas of care and mobility. Her communication was limited to crying to indicate displeasure; otherwise she kept quiet. Selvi reportedly very often cried whilst being fed and would turn her head away when her mother tried to wash her face. She was able to sit but she made no attempt to move or reach for objects. She was able to take a few steps with the support of her caregiver but frequently lifted her feet up from the floor.

Parental concerns and comments

Selvi's parents had very little understanding of her condition. Her mother was concerned about her poor eating habits and both parents were anxious that she should walk.

Assessment

Selvi was brought in to the Sensory Training Unit (STU) at Vidya Sagar.

The Sensory Training Unit assesses the needs of children and adults with profound and multiple disabilities. Students learn basic skills in communication and self-help and later as adults, may go on to enter the adult leisure programme where they are given a choice of activities, music, massage, relaxation in the hammock or a walk around the neighbourhood. The STU programme focuses on whole day management of the children, demystifying the condition for the family and caregivers and teaching basic skills.

These are children who will be dependent on another adult for their whole life, so the focus is also to help the child develop as much control over its environment as possible, and as many interactions with other people involved with its life and environment.

The initial process of assessment was through completing the classroom observation checklist for Selvi. She was observed in music therapy, education, while eating and also in her toilet habits. From these observations the classroom checklist and functional communication checklist could be completed.

The functional communication checklist reflected what had already been reported, namely, that Selvi cried to communicate displeasure, or kept quiet. An additional observation was that when put on a swing Selvi had in fact smiled and appeared very obviously to enjoy the sensation.

The initial observations also led to a hand function checklist being carried out which reflected that Selvi did not use thumb opposition with either hand, although she did try to reach out to some large objects within her base.

Observation of her eating mirrored the reports of her parents that she cried and turned away.

The physiotherapy assessment revealed that Selvi had slight hypomobility in all joints and mild hypotonia throughout her body. There were no contractures or deformities, nor were there any involuntary movements. She was able to maintain a sitting position quite easily with a fair amount of balance, but would not reach out of her base or move between different positions. She was able to take her weight in standing but would lift her legs from the floor without warning.

The obvious next assessment to be done was a sensory perception assessment, which revealed hypersensitivity around her mouth and cheeks, on the soles of her feet and the palms of her hands.

In conclusion, it was felt that her delayed motor development was linked to her disturbed sensory development, rather than to the inability to carry out movements. She was unwilling to use the movement abilities she had to explore her environment. The low sensory development was preventing her from developing any independence in eating and her general discomfort and irritability were interfering with the development of her communication abilities. It was also observed, that there was too much help and handling by the caregiver, which was preventing Selvi's spontaneous exploration of her environment.

Strengths

The fact that Selvi did not have any contractures or deformities and was able to take steps with support showed that there was potential for her to develop her participation, if not independence, in gross motor activities.

Her smiling when she was put on a swing also revealed that she would be able to communicate likes and dislikes at least at some level.

Needs

A very significant need for Selvi was to reduce the hypersensitivity around her mouth, on the soles of her feet and the palms of her hands as this was obviously interfering with many of her daily activities, including communication.

Linked to this was the need to develop the ability to take weight on her feet reliably so that transfers could be made easier for caregivers.

Functional goals

In the long term it was hoped that Selvi would:

- allow her mother to wash her face,
- eat independently,
- walk with a mobility aid, and
- communicate her choices in classroom and home situations.

Specific objectives

Within the first six months of input it was hoped that the following would be achieved:

- Reduce sensitivity around Selvi's mouth so that she does not cry or turn away when her face is washed.

- Enable Selvi to touch her food and take it to her mouth.
- Enable Selvi to chew semi-boiled carrots when introduced at the side of her mouth.
- Reduce sensitivity of the soles of Selvi's feet so that she is able to take weight in standing reliably for two minutes.
- Enable Selvi to look at an object related to an activity that she likes when she wants to do that activity.

Activities

- Selvi to be shown a piece of rope from a swing, encouraged to touch it, then be placed in a swing and bumped against a padded wall, with varying intensity and direction.
- Firm rubbing with hard, smooth object on Selvi's feet, arms and hands prior to related activity, e.g., weight bearing, reaching, etc.
- Selvi to be seated on a balance board with feet placed firmly on the floor and encouraged/facilitated to rock/weight shift.
- Selvi to stand in an upright standing frame during classroom activities where appropriate.
- Facilitate Selvi to walk to the toilet with a caregiver following applying firm pressure to the palms and soles of feet.
- Firm rubbing of Selvi's cheek and around her mouth prior to eating.
- During play activities, such as, throwing, rolling or catching a ball, Selvi to be given the opportunity to shuffle her bottom and reach the object.
- Rough and tumble games.

In multi-sensory room

- Music to be played. When the music stops, Selvi to look at the machine, which should then be switched on again.
- Technique as above with coloured lights and also rattle sounds.
- Progress from this activity to presenting Selvi with two objects. Selvi is to look at the one that is switched on/making noise. Gradually progress to allowing Selvi to choose which one is to be switched on by waiting for her to look, then switching on that sound/light, etc.
- Prior to any of these activities Selvi should be given/shown the objects and allowed to touch and feel them.

Development of a communication aid

- A selection of objects relating to activities in Selvi's daily routine to be kept in a bag. Selvi to be encouraged to touch the object prior to the related activity, to allow anticipation and reduce anxiety/irritability. Gradually progress this method to Selvi making a choice about which activity she wishes to do.

Parent training

There were two main areas that initially needed to be addressed with Selvi's parents. First, they needed to understand her condition and realise how her problems were affecting her abilities. They already knew that she did not like being touched, but did not understand how it was linked to her other areas of development.

Second, the parents needed to understand the importance of giving Selvi the opportunity to explore her environment and then begin making choices.

Outcome

After a few months of input, both at school and from parents at home, Selvi was much less irritable and her crying had significantly reduced.

She is feeling her food but as yet not taking it to her mouth independently.

She walks to the toilet with a walking frame, guided by her caregiver who moves it forward for her.

Selvi has started to communicate using objects related to her daily routine.

She now responds to her name and participates in group activities. She is also enjoying painting, holding the brush and making marks on the paper.

How to progress

As her goals have not been fully achieved the programme will continue to work on the same areas. However, progress is definitely being made, so the same techniques will continue to be used. These techniques can then be tried in other areas of her daily routine, like dressing, to encourage her to take as active a part as possible in her daily care.

The difference Transdisciplinary working has made

Although Selvi would have had a daily routine within the STU, prior to the Transdisciplinary way of working there would have been more focus on physiotherapy. A lot more time would probably have gone into facilitating movement patterns, encouraging sequencing between positions, balance, etc. However, none of these would have been successful if the sensory issues had not been addressed. Selvi did not in fact have problems of abnormal movement patterns. It was more that she did not use the movement abilities she had due to fear of moving around in her environment. In this case her irritability and tolerance of handling has improved quickly through approaching her needs from a sensory angle, and this in turn has led to an improvement in movement abilities.

Subhiksha

Subhiksha was five-and-a-half years old when she first came to Vidya Sagar for assessment. She comes from a large middle class joint family, which included her grandmother, and five uncles and their families. She had already been diagnosed with athetoid cerebral palsy but had not received any input apart from acupuncture. (The doctor carrying out the acupuncture had promised that she would walk in three months.)

Initial presentation

At the age of five the life roles that would be expected would be playing with friends, communicating with family and friends, and attending school. Instead Subhiksha was mainly an observer of family life. She was fully cared for by her grandmother, which unfortunately meant that she was not being encouraged to be independent. She was able to communicate her basic needs by pointing and had a verbal yes and no and a few other single words, but she was not communicating much apart from indicating basic needs like food, drink or the toilet.

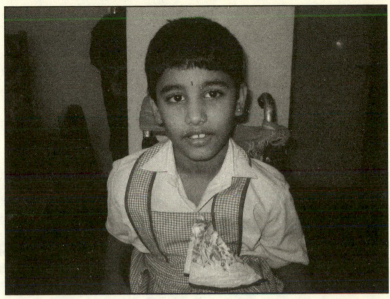

Subhiksha may be able to attend mainstream school soon.

Subhiksha although generally a happy child did not like being challenged, for example, being put in new unfamiliar postures, and she was reluctant to move around independently. She was happy to observe but not participate in group activities.

Parental concerns and comments

Subhiksha's mother was initially not keen to bring her to the Centre at all. She believed that Subhiksha would one day be all right and had faith in the acupuncture doctor's statement that she would soon walk. It was the father's initiative to bring her to Vidya Sagar; he wanted more information about her condition and what could be done. He too had very little understanding of her condition and expected spontaneous recovery.

She also had a caregiver at this time who was also reticent about bringing Subhiksha to Vidya Sagar as she was happy to be taking full care of her.

Subhiksha was brought into the home management programme and for the first few months was a very irregular attender. As the parents were so skeptical about receiving input from the Centre, the staff initially suggested they continue with the acupuncture but also allowed Subhiksha to take part in activities offered by Vidya Sagar.

When the acupuncture failed to make significant improvements in Subhiksha's condition, her father took the decision to discontinue it. Around this time the caregiver had to leave and so a new one was appointed. This lady was a parent of a child with special needs who had attended the home management programme until her son had begun to attend mainstream school. She, therefore, already had some insight into the issues surrounding Subhiksha and her family.

Assessment

Assessment began with the observation checklist, which was carried out in a modified way, as Subhiksha at this time was not in a class situation. However, from the observations made it was decided that a physiotherapy assessment, a hand function assessment and a functional communication assessment needed to be done.

As you would expect with athetosis, the physiotherapy assessment revealed that Subhiksha had involuntary movements and poor proximal stability. It was also observed that Subhiksha had more potential for movement than she was using. She was at this time able to sit independently on the floor but did not have dynamic sitting balance, tending to fall if she reached outside her base. It was felt that this was due to her over-handling and, therefore, lack of opportunity to move and explore her environment, leading to decreased sensori-motor experiences. There also appeared to be perceptual problems that were inter-linked with her reluctance to explore the environment. It was also observed that she had reduced awareness of her left side.

The hand function assessment revealed that she had good hand function when placed in a stable sitting position.

The functional communication checklist had led the therapist to carry out a receptive language assessment to assess her comprehension level. This reflected that her limited communication skills were due to lack of opportunity to communicate rather than a lack of understanding.

Strengths

Subhiksha was already able to communicate her basic needs, and was vocalising a few single words, showing that there was definitely potential to increase her communication skills. She had good hand function and could maintain sitting on the floor independently also, again indicating that she had potential to develop her movement abilities.

Needs

Subhiksha needed primarily to be given an opportunity to explore her environment and communicate with others. She also had more specific needs obviously, for example, to increase proximal stability, but those were needs linked to her lack of movement experiences.

Her poor perceptual and sensory perception was also linked to the lack of opportunity to move.

Functional goals

In the long term it was hoped that Subhiksha would:

- Understand and express simple concepts and ideas.
- Move between different positions and around the room independently.
- Walk with a walking frame.
- Become independent with her ADLs (activities of daily living, e.g., washing, dressing, etc.).

Specific objectives

After three months of input Subhiksha would be able to do the following:

- Begin using prepositions, direction and adjectives in simple sentences.
- Move independently between lying, sitting and high kneeling.
- Use her left hand to reach out of base for an object.
- Use some means of independent mobility to move between rooms at school (home management department) and at home.

Activities

- Gross motor activities including using therapy ball to facilitate good movement patterns, increase muscle tone, improve joint stability and increase confidence when moving through space.
- Action songs to introduce concepts, increase vocabulary, etc.
- Picture matching activities.
- Use of standing (supported as necessary) as a posture during education activities to increase muscle tone and give experience of anti-gravity postures.
- Facilitated walking between sessions within school and around home.

Parent training

After appointing a new caregiver there were quite rapid changes in Subhiksha's abilities. The new caregiver had experience of handling and so was able to judge how much support to give and how much to challenge Subhiksha to do on her own. Subhiksha quickly gained confidence and realised what she should be doing, and how much she could in fact do.

She was only attending Vidya Sagar twice a week at this point, and on the other days the programme was being carried out at home.

As far as the parents were concerned, they were slowly convinced about the programme as they saw their daughter begin to explore her environment, attempt things on her own, get on and off a chair and communicate more thoughts and feelings. She also started eating independently. Her programme was always very functional and an important part was teaching the parents what was appropriate for her age. They had still been treating her as a baby, putting her on a potty in front of other family members up until this point. They had to realise she was growing up. She was soon getting on and off the potty herself.

Her mother was still a bit reticent, but was happy to let her continue with the programme as she could see the improvements. She herself did not attend any sessions at home management for over six months.

After six months Subhiksha started coming daily to home management, and her mother started attending parent-teacher meetings. In the first year, when it was the school's annual day and Subhiksha took part in the celebrations, her mother was very upset that her daughter had been on stage in a wheelchair. But the following year she helped make costumes and brought relatives along to the performance.

Outcome

As can be seen from the earlier section, there was a big change in both Subhiksha's abilities and also in her parents' understanding of her condition. She quickly started to cooperate with the programme, helped by the fact that all activities were made fun and her teacher (Transdisciplinary worker) respected what Subhiksha was happy with and moved her on as she was ready. It was not long before she was able to walk with assistance. By this time she was also independent with many ADLs.

Communication was also improving simultaneously. For all new activities there were picture symbols, new words and commands, which were increasing her vocabulary. She is now able to communicate and complete classroom work at a Grade 1 level by using her communication chart.

She has moved into the reception class in the day centre and is managing very well. She uses a chart for communication, uses crawling for mobility around the classroom and sits comfortably on an ordinary classroom chair.

How to progress

Subhiksha is a very bright child and has made rapid progress in all areas since the programme was started. The hope is that she will be able to attend mainstream school in the near future, although the staff are aware that her mother, who has finally become comfortable with and confident of everyone at Vidya Sagar, may take some time to accept this new proposal.

The difference Transdisciplinary working has made

Subhiksha's programme was very functional and integrated all her needs right from the beginning. For example, she was working on sequencing between positions independently and developing her perceptual skills at the same time, which enabled her to quickly achieve climbing on and off the potty independently. If her needs had been separated out into perceptual needs and physical needs, she would probably have spent time working on strengthening around her hips by use of a variety of postures and activities. To then transfer these skills to a functional task would probably have taken a new set of activities and therefore been more time consuming. Also, communication was being worked on during all sessions and activities with new vocabulary being introduced all the time, again making progress that much quicker and relevant.

Raqeeb

Raqeeb is a ten-year-old boy with a metabolic disorder that is causing him global developmental delay and mental retardation. When he first came to Vidya Sagar he had previously only had medicinal input, with limited success. He comes from a well-educated upper middle class joint family, but he has no siblings. His condition seems to be familial, as there is a family history of several uncles also having disabilities. His mother had a miscarriage not long before coming to Vidya Sagar and had been told that it is not possible for her to have any more children.

Initial presentation

Raqeeb came across as a totally dependent, passive child. He was not acknowledging the presence of other people in the room at all. His only form of communication was to protest if he didn't like something, or smile if he was contented. He had no way of communicating yes and no. He had some visual problem and was not responding to visual stimuli. He had very little active movement, although he was able to come to sitting independently and would at times rock in this position. He did show some limited response to auditory stimuli.

His diet was an area of concern, particularly for his mother. He was on some kind of monthly cycle. The first week he would eat solids, the second week he would eat semi-solids, the third week only liquid and the fourth week only water.

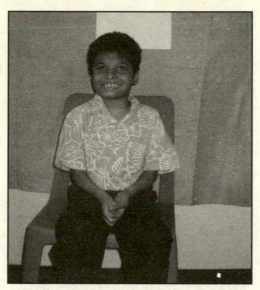

Raqeeb now responds well to familiar people.

Parental concerns and comments

Both parents realised it was a serious condition and their initial request was for an assessment and help with his dietary problems. They were quite realistic about his problems.

Assessment

Assessment began with observation, but as Raqeeb was so passive, responding to so little in his environment, little was gained by purely observing. Mallika (Transdisciplinary worker) felt that she needed to get to know him in order to understand him better. She carried out a physiotherapy assessment, which revealed no contractures or deformities. If placed in a sitting position he was able to balance independently; however he showed no inclination to move himself between positions, or reach out into his environment.

Through doing the physiotherapy assessment, Mallika was able to observe that Raqeeb was turning to sound and light and expressed discomfort by making a sound. From watching his mother feeding him she also concluded that he was sensory defensive around his mouth.

Strengths

Raqeeb was very tolerant of handling and in fact seemed to enjoy the vestibular and proprioceptive stimulation of being moved. Considering this along with the fact that he was able to sit independently implied there was some potential to develop his movement abilities by consistently using good handling techniques.

His use of sound to communicate displeasure and pleasure also indicated a potential to further his communication skills.

Needs

Raqeeb needed to develop his interaction with his environment in order to become less passive. This included maximising his movement potential and encouraging him to explore his environment, and of course, developing his basic skills in communication to a level where he could at least express yes and no, enabling him to begin to make some choices about his life where possible.

Another important need was to improve his dietary habits.

Functional goals

It is hoped that in the long term Raqeeb will be able to achieve the following abilities:

- Understand simple commands/questions/sentences related to his daily routine and body parts.
- Use vision and other senses to identify familiar people/objects.
- Move independently between postures on the floor.
- Have some independent means of floor mobility.
- Develop a more regular eating pattern, including solids, at least once a day.

Specific objectives

It was hoped that after three months, Raqeeb would have achieved the following:

- Indicate through touch, association between word and object/body part.
- Look at a coloured light and track it through 180 degrees.
- Sequence between lying and sitting independently.

- Roll independently from one end of the mat to the other.
- Experience changes of posture regularly (at least five times a day), throughout the day to give experiences of weight bearing, proprioceptive feedback and vestibular stimulation.

Activities
- Facilitation of various movement patterns, including rolling and side lying to side sitting.
- Tracking of coloured light in different postures.
- Action songs in front of mirror associating names with body parts or objects.
- Swinging—Raqeeb to be placed in bed sheet and swung from side to side.
- Four-point kneeling over a bolster, gently rocking backwards and forwards to give weight-bearing sensation through shoulders and hips.
- Sitting on a balance board with feet on floor and hands at either side of body, resting on balance board. Raqeeb to be rocked slowly from side to side to facilitate weight bearing through arms and also saving reactions.

Parent training

As Raqeeb's mother already understood that this was a serious condition, and had realistic expectations of her son, she took a lot of pleasure from seeing even the smallest improvement or evidence of a response from Raqeeb. She quickly understood why activities were being done and carried out the programme religiously at home, readily making equipment as suggested.

Outcome

Mallika found that whilst working with Raqeeb she quickly got to understand him better. Through repetitively facilitating gross motor activities she soon found that he would start to participate in the movement and after a couple of months would begin to initiate a movement himself. Mallika was able to move on from one movement pattern to a new one every few months.

Alongside this, Mallika was also introducing communication in the form of commands. Using the same movement and same command repeatedly until one day he began to respond to the command, rather than the movement by protesting if she said something he did not like or did not want to do.

Through use of a therapy ball Mallika made a breakthrough with developing a yes and no response. She was using the ball to give vestibular and proprioceptive input, and Raqeeb particularly liked to be bounced. She would say 'bounce' repeatedly with the activity, and when they stopped he would clap his hands. So then she said that if he wanted to bounce he had to clap his hands. This was the first time he responded like this. It was a big breakthrough.

The same simple greeting was used every session and eventually he started to turn hearing his name and smile. Then he began to try and make eye contact with his parents, caregiver and Mallika.

The diet cycle spontaneously broke somehow and he now eats solids on a daily basis.

His medication has also been reviewed and his convulsions are well controlled now. This has also improved his sleep pattern, with him awake during the day, obviously contributing to his ability to take part more actively in his daily routine.

Raqeeb is now able to maintain a variety of postures with only minimum support which is helping him develop strength and balance and cooperate in ADLs.

How to progress

Various doctors have told Raqeeb's mother that Raqeeb's condition is progressive and that he is living on borrowed time, an issue which is understandably stressful for the mother. However, he does not appear to be deteriorating at the moment, maintaining health, so the programme continues progressing as he shows responses.

He has recently had a visual assessment and is looking at and responding to patterns, so the programme now also incorporates encouraging him to use his vision and explore his environment. The yes and no response he has developed for therapy activities needs to be generalised more to other situations, but hopefully this will not be too difficult as he is now interacting more actively with more people.

Also, working on incorporating the movement abilities he has developed into his daily routine will help his mother and caregiver to care for him and allow him some control over his life.

The difference Transdisciplinary working has made

All areas of Raqeeb's management were being addressed from the start. As Mallika had knowledge in all areas, she was able to assess his communication and sensory needs while carrying out his movement programme. If his programmes had been separated out it would have been difficult to establish a baseline from which to start, as Raqeeb was not responding to anything or anyone in his environment. Through having only one worker Raqeeb was able to establish rapport with his therapist and she was able to understand his needs more clearly and move on with the programme more quickly.

Sriram

Sriram is sixteen years old, with a twin brother, Sunderam. Both brothers have cerebral palsy, Sriram is spastic diplegic and Sunderam is spastic quadriplegic. They have both been attending Vidya Sagar for many years, and are in the Red House stream within the day centre. Red House classes are made up of children with some degree of learning difficulty and look more at exploring vocations for these children, with less focus on academics except what will be relevant to their lives. They do some basic maths and some reading, but look more at options like gardening, cooking, and try to build on strengths the children have and what they are interested in.

Sriram's mother is a teacher at Vidya Sagar and one of the first Transdisciplinary trainees—Radha. The parents and the two boys live together in a small apartment and the extended family live nearby.

Initial presentation

Sriram is a wheelchair user, being able to propel himself around the school independently. He needed some help for most of his ADLs, although he actively participated in all activities.

Sriram is physically much more independent.

He had recently had surgery, bilateral hamstring release, prior to being taken on as a case study by Priya. His physiotherapy had been followed up for this surgery, taking place in the therapy room or at home, but there was little carry over into his daily activities. Language was felt to be his strength by his parents and the staff at Vidya Sagar as he was very verbal, but he had had little specific input in this area.

Socially Sriram enjoyed watching TV and liked to play cricket with some neighbours, preferring to bowl from his wheelchair, but also sometimes batting with the help of an adult. He enjoyed chatting with adults and participates in group games in class with supervision.

Parental concerns and comments

Both parents had a good understanding of his condition, and their main concern was to develop Sriram's level of independence, including his ability to walk and carry out his ADLs. They too did not feel that there were many problems with language.

Assessment

From observations within the classroom, a few specific assessments were found to be necessary, namely, visual perception, and social and interactive curriculum. It was observed that the reason for this was that Sriram was facing difficulties with scanning pages and his visual memory. He was also facing problems negotiating his wheelchair through spaces.

Further assessment found that he had poor body awareness, poor spatial orientation and had problems with abstract commands. All these were affecting his ability to carry out motor tasks, for example, dressing or moving independently from one place to another.

His physiotherapy assessment reflected the kind of picture you may well expect to find in a person with spastic diplegia, namely, fairly good upper limb function, independent sitting balance, the ability to stand and to take steps with support from a walker. However, he was not achieving as much independence as you would think his potential to be, due to the previously mentioned problems with spatial orientation, visual perception and difficulty in following commands. It was found that Sriram was scared to try out something new without some facilitation the first time, for example, throwing and catching a ball. Although physically he was very capable of balancing and had the range of movement needed in order to reach for the ball he was initially very reluctant to try.

There were also problems with communication, which mainly showed through Sriram becoming frustrated when he either did not understand someone or was not understood himself.

Observation revealed that his speech was usually very repetitive and the language he used was not age appropriate. He also had limited attention in a group setting.

Strengths

Sriram was very motivated to be independent and enjoyed social interaction whenever possible. He had good potential in terms of motor abilities with proper facilitation, and so it was hoped that with the correct approach in terms of strategies to cope with his specific difficulties, a high level of independence would be achievable.

Needs

Sriram needed to develop his communication skills, including the grammar and vocabulary he used, to develop his eye-hand coordination and spatial awareness and to learn strategies that enabled him to carry out tasks independently.

Functional goals

It was hoped that in the long term Sriram would:

- Be independent in the majority of his activities of daily living.
- Communicate effectively and appropriately with familiar adults.

Specific objectives

Within three months, it was hoped that Sriram would have achieved the following abilities:

- Learn a particular strategy for putting on trousers and shirt.
- Look at particular objects and reach out to them when presented with a functional task.
- Carry out a task in his daily routine following verbal instructions only. No physical prompts.
- Maintain a conversation with an adult by asking at least three appropriate questions.
- Make eye contact with the person who is speaking when in a group and recall what he has said or done.
- Use tenses in a sentence when conversing.

Activities

Eye-hand coordination activities that can be done in various settings, in various postures:

- Cutting vegetables and transferring them to a container.
- Holding a bowl and mixing.
- Passing things around to people.
- Throwing/catching a ball.
- Bowling with specific coloured pins to aim at.

Proprioceptive/body awareness activities:

- Use of therapy ball or balance board during reaching activities, in sitting or in lying positions.
- Crawling in and out of mazes/through furniture.
- Using different parts of his body to do different things (within creative movement sessions).
- Inset puzzles and copying simple block patterns.

Games to work on communication skills:

- Playing 'Simon says' within a group, taking turns to give instructions.
- 'Chinese whispers'—passing on a message.
- 'Charades'—guessing the word or action.
- To look at a person/picture and guess what the person is saying or feeling.
- Role plays—interviewing someone, planning a party/picnic, travelling by bus or train and shopping.
- Narrating events that have happened during the day.
- Describe a picture showing a sequence of events.
- Talking about recipes (simple steps) just followed.

Parent training

As Radha undertook the Transdisciplinary training course she gained a lot of insight into her son's needs. Some of her comments can be read in Chapter 5. The biggest change this insight made to her management of both her sons was incorporating their therapy into the daily routine and teaching them strategies and particular methods for doing their functional tasks.

Outcome

The greatest impact that this programme seemed to make was that it enabled Sriram to use the physical skills he had during his daily routine rather than thinking that physical activities were only to be carried out in the therapy room. Radha now says that she is able to give verbal prompts from another room to help Sriram carry out his tasks rather than needing to be physically around him all the time.

Consequently, he is now far more independent for most activities and manages to transfer himself independently at school, although his spatial awareness difficulties continue to be a problem at times. His planning skills have also improved with him realising that when school begins early in the morning, he will have to get up earlier in order to get everything done to be at school in time. It may seem like a small step, but it was a very significant one for Sriram.

The difference Transdisciplinary working has made

The fact that one person has been assessing Sriram from all angles has meant that it has been noted how much his proprioceptive difficulties are interfering with his use of his physical abilities to carry out his activities of daily living. From this conclusion, it has been possible to change his programme to address these needs appropriately, ensuring more success than previous programmes.

Sridhar

Sridhar is sixteen years old and lives with his parents and one brother. The family are of low socio-economic status, the mother work-ing as an ayah and the father as a gardener. Sridhar loves to be with his family and is keen to be as independent as possible. He has hemiplegic cerebral palsy and mild learning difficulties. He attends Vidya Sagar's day centre and is in the Red House stream, where the concentration is mainly on vocational skills. Sridhar is interested in gardening and during the holidays he often accompanies his father to work.

Sridhar takes an active part in the classroom.

Initial presentation

Sridhar is independently mobile although he walks with a pronounced limp and is unsteady on uneven surfaces. He is independent for all his ADLs. He is non-verbal although he does use some vocalisation along with gestures to communicate. He has a communication chart, but does not use it as often as he could; he tends to feel he doesn't need it.

Parental concerns and comments

Sridhar's parents have a good understanding of his condition and a lot of confidence in Vidya Sagar. Their main concerns are helping Sridhar to communicate more effectively and to develop a vocation.

Assessment

The assessments carried out for Sridhar were physiotherapy, hand function and communication.

The physiotherapy assessment indicated that generally Sridhar has poor proximal stability and uneven muscle tone in his trunk, which is affecting his balance and coordination during gait. His poor shoulder stability also affects his hand function. He is right hand dominant, and using the left more for support as he has poor manipulation with the left hand and some degree of associated reactions.

Various assessments were used to assess Sridhar's communication skills, including the social and interactive curriculum as well as the receptive and expressive language assessments. The findings were that Sridhar had difficulty initiating conversation, asking questions and socialising. Both his expressive and receptive language was at the four-word level. It was also found that his chart needed to be reorganised, updated and increased in order to encourage him to use it more.

Another interesting finding during these assessments was that it evidently took Sridhar quite some time to process and organise a command or instruction. From this it was decided to do a sensory perceptual assessment. This revealed no problems with visual, tactile, olfactory or gustatory sensory perceptions, but that generally he had a low arousal state and needed to be more active and alert to respond to his environment effectively.

Strengths

Sridhar is very motivated and already has a high level of independence. He has a good memory and has demonstrated good problem solving skills when it has come to developing gestures for communication.

Needs

Sridhar primarily needs to increase his need and ability to communicate. These two needs are closely linked. As Sridhar refines his communication skills and they become more effective, he will hopefully feel more confident and motivated to communicate in more situations.

He would also benefit from improving his balance and gait pattern along with his hand function.

Functional goals

It is hoped that in the long term Sridhar will achieve the following abilities:

- Travel independently to and from school. (He is currently escorted by his parents, which he dislikes.)
- Learn to play cricket and organise it with his friends.
- Organise and set up a school kitchen garden.

Specific objectives

Within three months Sridhar should have achieved the following abilities:

- Use his communication chart without prompt from an adult within the classroom and with friends.
- Explain an idea or plan to an adult, using his communication chart or gestures.
- Balance in a variety of postures (e.g., high kneeling, half-kneeling) and catch a ball thrown to him, reaching out of his base.

Activities

The programme addressing his physical needs consisted of a self directed exercise routine to increase his general state of alertness and to also work on his balance skills, for example, using the balance board or balance beam.

He was encouraged to use his communication chart at all times and the creative movement department, in particular, introduced a lot of games using his communication chart, for example, dumb charades and sabotage games.

Overall activities tended to be fast and challenging to increase his level of alertness, which proved to enhance his performance in general.

Parent training

As his parents already had a good understanding of his condition, the main point at this stage was to encourage them to allow Sridhar some more independence, encourage him to communicate more and to continue to challenge him at home as the staff were doing at school.

Outcome

Although it has not been long since the new programme has been introduced for Sridhar, there have already been noticeable improvements. His communication in the form of gestures has greatly improved and he takes a far more active part within the classroom, retelling incidents that have occurred rather than just waiting to be asked a question. His increased confidence in himself is helping his parents to have confidence in him too. He is enjoying his gardening and takes full responsibility for the plants he is growing at school.

The difference Transdisciplinary working has made

Sridhar's asymmetrical gait and poor balance immediately stand out; however, as documented above, he is in fact functionally mobile and independent in many skills. The finding that his general alertness needed to be increased provided a new insight and meant that the physical exercises that were carried out could be done so more effectively by making them more challenging and stimulating. This is different from what had been tried before, with exercises being moderated to prevent associated reactions becoming a problem. Also, by looking at Sridhar holistically, more importance was given to his communication needs—a very significant fact, relevant to someone of his age who will soon be leaving the day centre and will need to communicate effectively with people who have less understanding of his condition.

In conclusion, the change in approach to Sridhar's management meant that priorities of intervention were more clearly understood and appropriate.

Harishangar

Harishangar (Hari) is a bright thirteen-year-old boy; he attends the day centre at Vidya Sagar and is in the Green House stream where the classes work towards academic examinations. He has quadriplegic cerebral palsy and is a wheelchair user. He lives with his parents and younger sister. His mother works at Vidya Sagar in the speech therapy room and has a lot of experience working alongside speech therapists. She has also undergone some of the speech therapy training carried out by Ruth Duncan.

Hari has many interests, including listening to music, watching TV, taking part in quizzes and he is, like the majority of his peers, a big cricket fan.

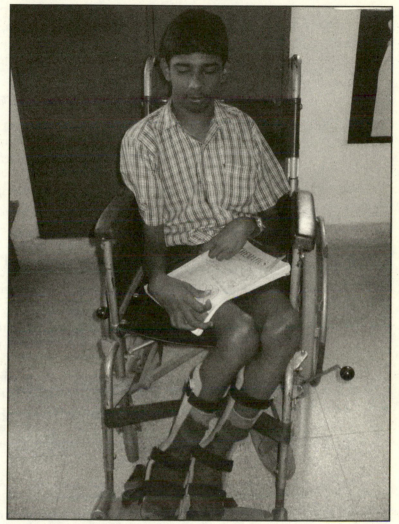

Hari studying hard for exams.

Initial presentation

As already stated, Hari is a wheelchair user, dependent for help with most of his ADLs. However he is aware of what help he needs and when to ask for it. He is motivated and with good facilitation will carry out all tasks as independently as possible. He is verbal though soft spoken, which means it is sometimes difficult for him to attract attention. His hand function is limited, which means that he is not able to self-propel his wheelchair. His writing skills are also limited; however this problem is overcome to a degree by using a computer in class, although this is too slow. He wears glasses and has bilateral nystagmus.

Parental concerns and comments

Hari's parents have a good understanding of his condition and their main concerns are for Hari to develop some degree of independence in his ADLs. They are also keen for him to be able to achieve his full potential academically, which involves looking at his access to education and developing his computer skills.

Assessment

After the initial observations were completed, more thorough assessments were carried out for Hari in physiotherapy, language, visual perception, and hand function. A separate seating assessment was also done.

The physiotherapy assessment reflected that Hari has increased muscle tone that increases very significantly with effort. This affects his balance and of course limits his active range of movement. The increase in muscle tone in his upper limbs affects his hand function and also his ability to use his arms and hands for balance, or even independent transfers. As effort has such a considerable effect on his muscle tone, adaptations that make a task easier along with good handling are important for Hari to develop his movement potential.

These same factors have some impact on his speech also. His voice is quiet and his sentences tend to be short, probably linked again to the effect that effort has on his muscle tone. As he makes the effort to speak his increased muscle tone will limit his ability to control his breath for speech.

Hand function again is limited by the fluctuations in tone associated with effort.

The assessment of visual perception revealed that Hari has difficulty in scanning horizontally, finding vertical scanning easier.

As may well be expected the seating assessment indicated that Hari needed to be provided with better proximal stability, a factor that would then influence all the areas above. Once provided with better proximal stability the effort needed from Hari is considerably reduced, enabling him to use his hands better, scan better and communicate with less effort.

Strengths

Hari is obviously a bright boy, with good cognition. He is motivated enough to develop all areas of his independence and tries to manage with the least amount of help necessary. With good handling techniques (i.e., with support being given appropriately to minimise effort) Hari has fairly good patterns of movement.

Needs

Hari needs to maximise his movement potential in order to become as independent as possible with his ADLs. This will also involve looking at providing adaptations that limit the effort needed from Hari.

Hari also needs to improve his communication skills so that he can communicate in a way that will benefit him functionally, and he can socialise more effectively. These skills will enable Hari to access a computer more successfully and so fulfil his academic potential.

Functional goals

In the long term it is hoped that Hari will achieve the following abilities:

- Take 10th standard exam on the computer in two years' time.
- Find out more information about his hobbies and interests through reading.
- Gain independence in toiletting.

Specific objectives

Within six months the following abilities should have been achieved by Hari:

- Maintain good posture whilst typing for five minutes.
- Increase sentence length by using conjunctions, and by increasing vocabulary.

- Be able to look at a whole piece of information and pick out five important points.
- Transfer independently from chair to wheelchair, and wheelchair to toilet.
- Sit and stand independently with support from bar in front.
- Side step five steps independently with front support from bar.
- Use voice or bell to call for help.

Activities

- Postures that can be used during day:

  - Prone standing frame
  - Side sitting
  - Prone lying
  - Sitting in adapted seat

- Adaptations that need to be made:

  - Proximal stability support in classroom seat
  - Jet for toiletting
  - Wall bars for support in bathroom
  - Dressing—velcro fasteners, press studs
  - Bathing—back scrubber, mirror
  - Gross motor activities to work on proximal stability, sequencing between positions, weight bearing and balance.
  - Computer games to work on scanning.
  - Access to own dictionary.

Parent training

As Hari's mother works at Vidya Sagar, she has a good understanding of his problems. The main purpose of parent training in this instance was to help them make the adaptations necessary within the home, and develop a programme that incorporated the activities listed into his daily routine.

Outcome

Many adaptations have been made in the home which are helping Hari's independence. Unfortunately, there have not been the physical improvements that were hoped for but this is probably due to a recent growth spurt, which has meant that Hari's muscles have become tighter. He is currently being reviewed by the medical team to decide what action to take. His reading and scanning skills have however improved and he is working well towards his exams.

The difference Transdisciplinary working has made

The main difference that the change in approach made in this case was that the link between Hari's communication difficulties and increased muscle tone due to effort was identified. This altered the priorities of treatment, as it was understood more clearly that adaptations would help Hari to communicate effectively. Previously it had been decided that too many adaptations were preventing Hari from achieving his movement potential. This change in approach reflected more clearly where Hari's potential lay, and therefore, what areas of input should be a priority.

Nagaraj

Nagaraj is a nine-year-old boy who comes from a family which is of low socio-economic status. He lives with his parents and older brother in a one roomed house. He has spastic quadriplegia and attends Vidya Sagar's day centre. He is in the Green House stream, where he is working on academics.

Initial presentation

Nagaraj is a bright boy, but with severe movement difficulties, causing him to be dependent for all aspects of self-care. He is a wheelchair user and needs fully supportive seating to enable him to lift his head. He has significant problems eating, and so is very small for his age. His nutrition problems also seem to link with his limited attention span. He is non-verbal, but tries to vocalise to gain attention, and then smiles to indicate yes; he remains quiet and still to indicate no. He also has a communication chart which he does use at times. Nagaraj, despite all his difficulties, is a cheerful, friendly, sociable boy and enjoys games with his classmates.

Parental concerns and comments

Nagaraj's mother is predominantly concerned with his general health. He suffers from repeated chest infections due to the problems he has with chewing and swallowing. She also realises that his cognition is his strength and so is keen for him to achieve his full potential in academics.

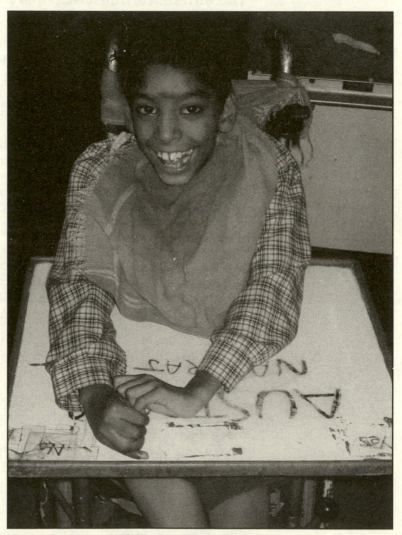

Nagaraj has success with his communication chart.

Assessment

Assessments were carried out in the following areas: physiotherapy, ADLs, hand function, communication, seating and eating.

The physiotherapy assessment revealed that Nagaraj has significantly increased muscle tone throughout his body, even at rest, which has a marked impact on all other areas of his development. The high tone severely restricts his active movements and he is developing asymmetrical postures that could become fixed deformities if there is no careful management. He lacks postural control in any anti-gravity position and his head control is limited to short periods of being able to raise his head when his body is fully supported in an adapted seat.

His seating assessment indicated that he needs support at all levels of his trunk and also the pelvis to try and control the developing scoliosis that will only cause more problems if allowed to progress.

His hand function is again very limited, although he does have some fairly wide range movements of the arms that enable him to point at his communication chart.

He is dependent for all ADLs, and this assessment concentrated on looking at handling issues and adaptations that would make the tasks as easy as possible for both Nagaraj and his mother.

His eating problems are related to his poor head control, bite reflex and lack of chewing ability. He needs food to be puréed and careful support of his head must be given to prevent choking.

Communication assessment revealed, as already stated, that he does have a yes and no response, but obviously this limits his communication enormously. He does point to his chart to make choices but at this stage his chart only has a few symbols on it and Nagaraj has difficulty accessing it due to his restrictions of physical movement.

Strengths

Nagaraj is a bright and cheerful person despite all his difficulties. He understands verbal instructions and is as compliant as possible.

Needs

For Nargis it is of primary importance to improve his general health and hygiene. This factor influences all other areas, as poor health and discomfort will further increase his muscle tone, which in turn will increase his poor head control and bite reflex, interfering with eating. All these factors will also reduce his ability to communicate.

As Nagaraj is so physically dependent, he needs a good postural management programme to prevent his physical difficulties impeding his progress in other areas more than necessary. Through good, supportive and comfortable postures that facilitate him to lift his head and use his arms, Nagaraj will be able to develop more effective communication. This will enable him to work more on his strengths, i.e., academics and participating socially with his peers. It is also vital that the development of contractures and deformities is minimised as much as possible.

As far as ADLs are concerned, at this stage Nagaraj needs to be helped to participate as much as possible in ADLs to make care for him more comfortable and less time consuming.

Functional goals

It is hoped that in the long term the following can be achieved:

- Improved general health and personal hygiene.
- Effective and meaningful communication skills.
- Improved quality of his social life.

Specific objectives

Within three months, the following is required to be done (some of these goals are ongoing, lifelong goals that are necessary to achieve the long-term functional goals):

- Investigate medical issues relating to his dietary problems.
- Improve the quality of the food he has.
- Have a postural management programme with hourly changes in posture throughout the day.
- Maintain ranges of movement throughout his body.
- Develop his proximal stability to improve his head control and maximise use of upper limbs and hands for communication, including developing shoulder stability to facilitate

accurate pointing to words and symbols on his communication chart.
- Introduce the alphabet and words to his communication chart.
- Work with his brother to develop his understanding of how to interact with Nagaraj so they can play together.
- Build on his interest in music so that he makes choices as to which cassette he wants to listen to.

Activities
- Meeting with doctors to discuss management of diet: possibility of gastrostomy, dietary supplements, and medications to help bladder and bowel control.
- Postural Management: postures that provide support, maintain ranges of movement and encourage development of proximal stability and head control:

  - Prone lying on prone board
  - Prone stander
  - Side lying
  - Supported seating

- Facilitated gross motor activities to maximise movement potential, and assist in transfers:

  - Rolling
  - Side lying to side sitting
  - Sit to stand

- Facilitated postures to help develop shoulder stability and upper limb active movement:

  - Weight bearing through arms in side sitting and four point
  - Reaching activities in supported sitting

- Development of language skills for both social interaction and academics:

  - Spelling of simple words
  - Word building games
  - Yes/no answer quiz games

- Scanning activities, picking out a specific word from choice of two similar words
- Picking out specific words from his chart

Parent training

His mother is being involved in the meetings and discussions with the medical team so that understanding of nutritional needs and ways of dealing with the problems Nagaraj has can be properly explained and addressed.

Outcome

Nagaraj has done well since the beginning of his Transdisciplinary programme. His eye pointing with his communication chart has vastly improved and he has begun to express opinions and ideas. As he has become easier to understand, he has become more motivated to communicate and has become less of a spectator when with his peers.

Nagaraj recently underwent biofeedback therapy that has greatly improved his head control and posture. This will hopefully also influence eating and therefore general health.

The difference Transdisciplinary working has made

Again in this instance, the main difference that the change in approach has brought has been in prioritisation. His movement needs have been given less priority and most of these needs being met through posture management. His communication needs have been given a higher priority and are addressed in each of the postures and in all of the different situations in which Nagaraj may find himself, overall providing a more comprehensive programme.

Rakesh

Rakesh is twelve years old and lives with his mother and three sisters. His father is away a lot as he is in the army. Rakesh is a bright boy with spastic diplegia and moderate hearing loss, who has been coming to Vidya Sagar since 1996. Initially he attended the home management programme and then moved on to the

Computer whiz kid.

day centre in 1998. He is studying for his National Open School exams in the Green House stream.

Initial presentation

Rakesh is a wheelchair user, which he self-propels very proficiently. He had a hamstring release a few years ago and is able to stand with support, but both knees buckle if he tries to take a step. His upper limb function is good, particularly fine hand movements, and he is independent for most ADLs with a little help required at times.

He is very sociable and initiates conversation with many people. He uses gestures and some vocalisation to communicate, although he also has a communication chart. He enjoys games with his peers and also painting and music.

Parental concerns and comments

His parents are mainly concerned with developing his stepping ability.

Assessment

A physiotherapy assessment was carried out to try and establish why Rakesh was unable to step more functionally. He is able to come to stand from sitting with front support independently, but the assessment revealed very poor quadriceps control and poor lateral weight shift that prevented him from stepping successfully. Another significant finding was that although his upper limb function is good, he has a slight contracture of his right shoulder that limits flexion. It appears that this stems from an operation to remove a nodule (it is not clear exactly what) when he was young, which has left scar tissue that consequently restricts movement. This contracture does unfortunately impede the stability of his right shoulder, limiting his ability to take weight fully on his upper limbs to assist in stepping.

Assessment of his communication skills reflected that Rakesh is a very active communicator. He does not like to give up and repeatedly uses gestures and single word vocalisations to try and get his point across. Unfortunately, he does not seem to appreciate how the communication chart could help him in situations where his other means of communication are not successful.

His fine hand function is good and he is able to manipulate small objects successfully.

There were no indications from the initial observations that Rakesh had any perceptual problems.

Strengths

Rakesh is bright and very motivated to communicate and be independent. He enjoys social interaction and initiates conversation very readily. His good hand function and the fact that he has no perceptual problems enable him to carry out the majority of his ADLs independently.

Needs

In order to become more independent in transfers, it would benefit Rakesh to develop his standing balance and weight shift to enable him to step independently, supporting himself with his hands.

His communication could be made more successful with refining his hand gestures and also encouraging him to use his communication chart.

Functional goals

In the long term it is hoped that Rakesh will achieve the following abilities:

- Transfer independently in all settings.
- Be able to communicate effectively in all circumstances.
- Achieve full potential in academics.

Specific objectives

Within six months Rakesh should be able to achieve the following:

- Improve standing balance so that he is able to stand, using one hand for support and reach out of his base with the other hand.
- Develop quadriceps control so that he is able to take ten steps forwards with a walker without his knees buckling.
- Improve listening skills so that Rakesh attends to a question fully before replying.
- Use specific/refined sign language to enhance communication.
- Use the communication chart without prompt from another person when not understood.
- Develop handwriting and computer skills.

Activities

- Gross motor activities to develop balance, weight shift, quadriceps control, shoulder strength and stability:

  - Sit to stand
  - Reaching in back-standing
  - Stepping on/off small step within parallel bars using upper limbs for support
  - Four point—weight shift and reaching

  - Pushing games/activities in kneeling or back standing—pushing large therapy ball, throwing a ball
  - Stepping practice—sideways, forwards with upper limbs providing support

- Activities to develop listening skills:

  - Increase sound awareness to different sounds in his environment: phone, cooker, doorbell, car

- Activities to increase attention to detail:

  - Spot the difference pictures and patterns
  - Quizzes

- Developing sign language:

  - Specific training in sign language
  - Fine motor activities to increase dexterity, painting, clay modelling

Parent training

Parent training in this instance is targeted towards encouraging them to help Rakesh to develop his communication skills, by increased use of his communication chart and also more specific gestures. They have also received training on specific handling techniques to use when assisting Rakesh with his transfers, facilitating him to develop greater independence.

Outcome

For Rakesh, since the introduction of his more integrated programme the main change has been observed in goals that he has set for himself. He seems to have realised that walking is not the most important thing for him as he is fully independently mobile with his wheelchair and able to transfer independently in most settings. He has begun to concentrate more on his communication and somehow his listening skills seem to have improved along the way too. He is very interested in computers and sees his future in this kind of work, whereas earlier all he wanted to do was play sport.

The difference Transdisciplinary working has made

Again the main difference has been made by prioritisation, with more importance being given to communication needs after realising that Rakesh was not communicating as effectively as possible. One also realised that this would have an impact on his independence, as it would affect his ability to ask for help when he needed it.

Sudha Mani

Sudha Mani is a thirteen-year-old girl with spastic diplegia. She lives in a remote village in a hilly location on the borders of Karnataka and Tamil Nadu. She is a Dalit girl, which means that she is in the lowest strata both socially and economically. She lives in a building that consists of two huts that have been joined to make one home. The terrain is very uneven and the house has different levels throughout. She lives there with her parents, siblings, uncle and his family; in all there are ten people living in the two huts.

Initial presentation

Sudha Mani is a very shy and passive girl. The CBR worker who had been working with her found it very difficult to gain her cooperation for any of the activities. She would bottom shuffle around the home and was totally dependent for all ADLs. She would watch her siblings playing but never took part and had no chores to do around the home. She had no education, although she was able to speak quite well with family and friends.

Parental concerns and comments

Sudha Mani's parents had no expectations of her and were generally resigned to her condition. They expressed a desire that she should be a little more independent with ADLs, but beyond that expectations were minimal.

Sudha Mani learns to come up to stand.

Assessment

Mallika (Transdisciplinary worker) found that the concept of life roles was a very useful place to start with Sudha Mani, her parents and the CBR workers who had been involved in her care so far. She found that the discussion changed their approach to Sudha Mani and led to a better understanding of her needs.

Following the initial discussion which explored Sudha Mani's expectations, various assessments took place to identify her specific needs more clearly.

The physiotherapy assessment revealed restricted ranges of movement which consequently affected her mobility and postures, although she was able to move between a number of positions independently.

The hand function assessment was carried out using all the items that Sudha Mani might use in her own home—her cup, plate, etc.—and it was quickly discovered that she in fact had the ability to eat independently. She was also able to hold a number of other functional objects purposefully.

No formal communication assessment was done at this time as she was able to communicate quite clearly through speech. Her social interactions were discussed as one realised that she had little interaction with her own peer group.

Her education was also discussed, although Sudha Mani expressed no desire to receive any kind of education and was in fact very un-cooperative with the CBR worker.

One large area of concern was her toiletting. Sudha Mani had to go to the toilet just outside the house, where there was no privacy for her.

Strengths

Sudha Mani was obviously a bright girl who had a good understanding of things happening around her. Her communication skills were good and she interacted well with her family. She also had good upper limb function, although this was not being used to its potential.

Needs

Sudha Mani needed to learn to use the skills she has to become more independent in her ADLs. She also required adaptations to be made to allow her to use the bathroom and toilet in privacy. A major need for Sudha Mani was to motivate her to develop an interest in herself and her future. She had so little expectations of herself that she was not achieving her potential. It was felt by those working with her that she needed to develop some vocational skill and also given some responsibilities around the house. Basic numeracy and literacy skills would also help her to become more independent and a more active member of the household.

A more specific therapy need was for her to have changes of posture regularly through the day to maintain ranges of movement and prevent the complications of contractures and deformities. It was also recognised that if she was provided with a wheelchair, once helped down to the road, she would be able to get into the village.

Functional goals

In the long term it is hoped that the following would be achieved by Sudha Mani:

- Be independent in toileting and ADLs.
- Be a contributing member of the family.

Specific objectives
In the next few months, the following should be achieved:

- Sudha Mani should be provided with a wheelchair and taught to use it independently once helped to the road.
- Specific postural changes should be taking place through-out the day to help maintain ranges of movement.
- Sudha Mani should be eating independently.
- Sudha Mani should have chores around the house, for example, setting places for eating, washing plates and helping to prepare food.
- Sudha Mani should have learnt simple concepts, such as, counting, money and time.
- Interactions with peers should be taking place and a role model for Sudha Mani identified.

Activities
- Postural management programme to maintain ranges of movement, and to provide suitable positions for the following activities.

All activities should be simple and short to give Sudha Mani a sense of achievement and pleasure in having finished a job.

- Beading
- Sorting vegetables
- Cleaning, washing and stacking vessels
- Using crayons and paint
- Stitching

- Wheelchair mobility skills
- Sitting with siblings and cousins

Parent training

The parent training in this case has focused on increasing the parents' expectations of Sudha Mani. They are being encouraged to assign her roles and responsibilities. They needed to be encouraged to see Sudha Mani as a thirteen-year-old and treat her accordingly in order for Sudha Mani to develop motivation to become more independent.

Outcome

Since the programme began many changes have occurred. Sudha Mani is making the most of her physical abilities, changing her posture and pulling to stand with assistance. She is also using the toilet adaptation that has been provided.

She quickly learnt how to use the wheelchair and goes around the village independently. She is already taking a more active role within the family.

How to progress

As Sudha Mani is making progress so quickly, it is hoped that she will soon have her own ambitions and be motivated to become more and more independent as she realises her own potential.

The difference Transdisciplinary working has made

Using the life roles approach really helped in this case as it prompted all those involved in Sudha Mani's life to see her as a developing young woman. This really changed the whole approach to her management and meant that the programme that was subsequently developed was meaningful and appropriate.

If Sudha Mani's problems had been looked at as separate issues, for example, from a purely physiotherapy point of view, her programme would probably not have been nearly so successful, as the main thing needed here was a holistic approach with development of expectations and personal motivation.

8 The Multidisciplinary Team

As the concept of a Transdisciplinary worker changes the model of working with children with disabilities (see Chapter 4), we felt it would be good to include in this book, some comments from members of the multidisciplinary team regarding the concept. First, we have input from two doctors, Dr Vishwanathan, consultant neurological paediatrician, and Dr Venkatramanan, consultant orthopaedic surgeon. Both these doctors have worked closely with members of the core team since they have undergone the Transdisciplinary training programme. They were asked about their opinions of the concept as a whole, and then about their individual experiences of the model from working with the core team members. They were also asked what they thought needed to be changed, improved or done differently, and how the concept could be taken further.

For input from other members of a multidisciplinary team there are comments from the three health trainers that initially trained the core team. All three come from the UK where the model of working is strongly along the lines of multidisciplinary team working, with clearly defined roles and responsibilities for each of the different professionals. The attitude of the professional bodies is to maintain the separate professions, with increasing specialisation and level of expertise in each particular field. With this in mind, the views of these three individuals who have been involved in developing the role of a Transdisciplinary worker should offer some insight into the benefits of this model. They all have a lot of experience of multidisciplinary working, enabling them to discuss possible reservations that health professionals may have about certain elements of Transdisiciplinary working.

Dr V. Vishwanathan, MRCP DCH

Dr Viswanathan graduated from Chennai in the year 1986. In 1987, he qualified in Paediatrics with a DCH and MRCP from UK. He then went on to acquire specialised training in paediatric neurology and became a member of the British Paediatric Neurology Association. He is also a member of the International Child Neurology Association, the Neurological Society of India and the Indian Academy of Paediatrics. He has a lot of experience in working with epilepsy, muscular dystrophy and other neuromuscular disorders. He returned to Chennai at the end of 1997 and is working as a consultant paediatric neurologist at the Kanchi Kamakoti Childs Trust Hospital, Sundaram Medical Foundation Hospital. He also has a private clinic.

Many parents are scared to ask doctors questions.

Dr Vishwanathan has worked with Vidya Sagar for a number of years, but more closely since the Transdisciplinary training has been completed as it is since then that a number of children have been selected and assessed for bo-tox injections. Clinics have been carried out jointly with Dr Vishwanthan, Dr Venkatramanan and the staff at Vidya Sagar.

Referrals regularly pass between the staff at Vidya Sagar, particularly the out-patients' department, but also the day centre and home management, and Dr Vishwanathan.

When asked what he felt about the concept of a Transdisciplinary worker, Dr Vishwanathan was positive that there was a role for this type of individual, particularly in countries like India where rural communities have limited access to the medical team. He felt that Transdisciplinary workers could offer parents the kind of support they need by being able to answer most questions and doubts that parents may have.

> Explaining to parents is a lot easier coming from a therapist. Many times, particularly here in India, people are too scared to ask doctors a question. They think their questions are stupid and they would rather ask someone they know better. The therapist may know them better (than the doctor).

> In cities, awareness and knowledge is higher, but when families come to me from villages the level of knowledge is often so low that it takes a huge amount of time for me to explain. The first session is so long. This could be cut down if someone like this (Transdisciplinary worker) is able to spend time with them answering their questions. People remember so little from their first appointment that they need the follow up for reinforcement of the importance of continuing with the drugs or whatever. Sometimes they don't come back to see me, as they haven't understood the importance of what I have been telling them. People like this (Transdisciplinary workers) are very helpful to reinforce and explain the need for input.

> — Dr V Vishwanathan

Dr Vishwanathan has been communicating a lot with Lakshmi, one of the core team members who is currently in charge of the out-patients' department. When asked about his experiences of working with Lakshmi, he again was positive, commenting that the referrals he now receives are more specific, with basic problems already noted and initial explanations already given to parents.

The good thing is that they (TD workers) seem to have their basics right. They can identify static disorders, progressive disorders, neuromuscular disorders, cerebral palsy and other disorders, which is good. I think many therapists don't understand these issues—where does the disorder lie—the muscle tissue, the brain, or the nerve? It really helps because it gives some background and I can go from there. Also, parents have been told there is a problem, and have had some explanation, which makes my job easier.

— Dr Vishwanathan

Dr Vishwanathan also described how keeping the communication channel open between himself and Vidya Sagar helped him to work more effectively.

Because the communication channel is open between us, Lakshmi calls me and asks questions so that she can then explain better to the parents. She is doing the kind of work that a health visitor or specialist nurse would do in the UK and that is really very good as it enables me to spend more time on clinical issues rather than the basics.

Another example is with seizures. I used to find parents stopping the baby's drugs because the baby was sleepy, but now I have tried to explain that the seizures are causing the sleepiness not the drugs, and Lakshmi is also explaining this, so they continue with the drugs and we get better results.

— Dr Vishwanathan

Dr Vishwanathan made a few recommendations regarding how to improve this model of working, or any changes that needed to be made:

Documentation/Communication
Although there are frequent telephone conversations discussing the children, a written feedback letter would be useful that could be filed in the notes, making it easier for him to know what input the child was getting from Vidya Sagar. In some cases he makes referrals to Vidya Sagar but hears nothing back. In these situations he is never sure if the child has been to Vidya Sagar for advice or not.

Level of knowledge
Although, as already stated, Dr Vishwanathan is impressed with the basic knowledge that the staff have, he now feels that the

depth of knowledge could be increased. When asked what areas in particular, it was discovered that they were in fact areas that had been covered in training and so it is very probably lack of experience and confidence in these subjects that is causing the Transdiscplinary workers to be more hesitant. This issue needs to be addressed by looking at time allocation, particularly for practical application during the training course itself.

Over-burdening!

In contrast to comments about Transdisciplinary working over-burdening one person with too much knowledge, the point being made here was that the staff at Vidya Sagar are overburdened because of the sheer number of referrals that are sent to them. The solution to this is obviously to have more people trained in this way so that comprehensive services can be offered to a greater number of people.

Dr Venkatramanan

Dr Venkatramanan studied at Grant Medical College, Bombay, to gain his MBBS and MS (Orthopaedics). Since then he has worked at Children's Orthopaedic Hospital, Bombay, where he was a registrar for one-and-half years and then as a lecturer in Topiwala National Medical College for four years. He subsequently moved to Chennai where he now works as a consultant orthopaedic surgeon at Sooriya Hospital.

Dr Venkatramanan has become involved with Vidya Sagar over the past two years, initially with clinics to assess and follow up children for bo-tox injections. The working partnership with Dr Venkatramanan has developed to a point where he now comes to the Centre on a more frequent basis and assesses children regarding the necessity for orthopaedic input. He has carried out surgery on a number of the children from the Centre and has worked closely with the Vidya Sagar staff regarding their follow up, ensuring good results from the surgical intervention.

When asked about his thoughts on the concept of a Transdisciplinary worker, Dr Venkatramanan agreed that it was a good idea and relevant to countries like India where the large numbers of rural communities have limited access to a multidisciplinary team. He was however sure that the multidisciplinary team was still a necessity.

> It's a very nice idea to identify one individual who will have a significant amount of knowledge about cerebral palsy, in these three fields (physio, speech and occupational therapy). But their level of knowledge should be a little bit more, but that is just from my perspective as an orthopaedic surgeon. But I think they are good at the integration level. They can start off a programme for a person and include all the important necessary things that the child needs. How far they will be able to do it on their own I don't know, and take it to what level and what degree before they find it is becoming difficult for them. It's something I am not able to say. You can't do without specially trained people (the multidisciplinary team). They have a higher level of knowledge and experience in certain areas because they are concentrating on just that area.
>
> – Dr Venkatramanan

As orthopaedic surgeons themselves work with the condition (cerebral palsy) on a specific level, they need to converse with professionals who have a high level of understanding of the condition. When someone has knowledge in more areas, and is managing all areas of a child, it is admittedly difficult to have such specialised knowledge in one area. The staff at Vidya Sagar are aware of this and this is why it has never been stated that this model of working negates the need for the multidisciplinary team. In fact, their skills and expertise can be utilised in a more efficient and effective way. When a Transdisciplinary worker has a query or doubt about a child's problems, they have to refer to the relevant health professional for specific advice and input (see Chapter 4).

Dr Venkatramanan also admits that in his experience there are few therapists with a high level of knowledge in cerebral palsy, echoing Poonam's comments in Chapter 1. In light of this he feels that time and experience will do a lot to develop the knowledge and understanding of the Transdisciplinary workers.

> I think that with all these things, it takes about five to six years to develop a high enough level of knowledge and confidence. The multidisciplinary team will always be necessary. To achieve the

best results for these children you will always need to cross over to the specialist at some point. Someone who spends all their time in one field will have more expertise in that area, so you need to tap into their knowledge. But in a country like ours where there is such a large number of patients, this is definitely a practical answer. You may also need to check with a specialist that you are not going down the wrong track, or missing something important. Knowing when to refer is so important

– Dr Venkatramanan

Interestingly, since moving to Chennai, Dr Venkatramanan has not found any therapists with good working knowledge of cerebral palsy, and in comparison, the staff from Vidya Sagar know a lot more, again reflecting Poonam's comments in Chapter 1.

Regarding his experience of working with the core team of Transdisciplinary workers, Dr Venkatramanan's comments were mostly around the issue of confidence. He feels that he had seen a change over the last two years in the team's understanding of technical jargon and terminology and they evidently understand him more clearly. However, he still feels that this area could be developed, so that the team are confident to initiate communication more readily, giving relevant background about the child and explaining clearly what they are working on with the child. At present, he finds it useful to have a physiotherapist who also knows the child present at the assessment clinics too.

The referrals that are made to him are on the whole appropriate, with a few being referred possibly earlier than really necessary, but this is obviously preferable to them being referred too late.

Initially I didn't feel they understood what I was saying, but now it is much better. When I say something they do understand what I am trying to say—this muscle group is tight or whatever—initially they had some doubts. Now when I say it they are very sure about what the problem is and what we need to do now. But I would like more input from them. I feel sometimes that they know there is a problem but are not able to communicate clearly—they need to be more specific. They are not forthcoming enough. Maybe I haven't been good at asking the right questions to get an overall perspective of the child, how far the parents understand and what they are expecting and what are their aims of input. That needs to be communicated better. With more information like that I will

be able to focus better on what I need to look at rather than doing a quick assessment of all different postures.
                                                            – Dr Venkatramanan

To take this model of working further, Dr Venkatramanan had some specific ideas from his position as an orthopaedic surgeon:

Level of knowledge
In order to help the team develop their confidence when discussing specific issues with members of the medical team, it will help if their level of knowledge is slightly more. This is particularly relevant when it comes to anatomy. This subject is covered in the training course, but obviously in far less depth than a physiotherapist or doctor would have during their training. Although the aim is not to produce a physiotherapist at the end of the course, Transdisciplinary workers do need to understand the importance of a good grounding in basic anatomy and the relevance of it in their management of children with special needs. Their level of understanding needs to be such that they can communicate clearly and effectively with the medical team.

Documentation/Communication
Echoing the comments of Dr Vishwanathan, Dr Venkatramanan emphasised the need for adequate notes to be kept for the children. This is particularly important for children undergoing surgery to ensure information is relayed correctly between those people involved in the child's care after surgery. This helps ensure that programmes are carried out properly to gain maximum benefit from the intervention, and also, any problems that arise can be dealt with quickly and effectively. Communication is also vitally important with surgery as sometimes the aims of an orthopaedic surgeon can be vastly different from a parent's aims, and this needs to be clarified and discussed.

Confidence
This is a small point that has already been touched upon. It takes time and experience for knowledge to be consolidated in any subject, and so for the Transdisciplinary team to feel confident in their abilities is not going to happen overnight; however, already in the two years that Dr Venkatramanan has worked with Vidya Sagar, he has seen a difference.

In conclusion, Dr Venkatramanan was in agreement with Dr Vishwanathan about the role of a Transdisciplinary worker in countries like India.

It is a very good concept for a country like ours where it is difficult to get the whole multidisciplinary team to assess a child at the same time and parents' education level may not be adequate enough to grasp all the concepts. In India you need this kind of person who can answer at least most of the questions that will be raised by parents. People who can instill some confidence in these parents, say 'yes, your child can do this, what you are doing is logical'. If the parents have this kind of input and see progress with the child they will carry on with the programme. Without a proper programme the parents will lose interest.

–Dr Venkatramanan

The Therapy Trainers

Kate Tebbett—Physiotherapist

My experiences in the UK have been of working in a multidisciplinary team, based in a hospital, with visits out into the community. I worked at a child development centre where it was relatively easy to discuss your cases with other members of the medical team. We tended to try and set joint goals, but I think because sessions with the children were on the whole separate therapy sessions, there was a limit to the amount of integration between the therapy programmes. As Poonam described in Chapter 1, I am sure many of the parents I worked with in the UK would have felt inundated with programmes and instructions from all the different health professionals.

When I first arrived at Vidya Sagar in 1999, I had limited understanding of the health issues faced by people living in a country such as India. I also had some reservations about the project, mainly along the lines of whether it was reasonable to train one individual in so many areas of expertise, and expect them to be able to handle all aspects of a child's care. However, as time went on I began to understand how this type of professional—a Transdisciplinary worker—would be invaluable in developing countries such as India. As I began the training of the core team, I realised how their years of experience working with the families of children with special needs helped them to quickly understand the therapy that I was teaching them. If I described a certain condition, posture or type of movement they were immediately able to picture it and relate specific problems they knew were related to that condition or posture. It made training them very easy. They took things on board and gradually began to try them out. Obviously confidence only comes with time, and so their expertise is still developing. However, I am confident that they are clear with the basic principles and can work from there. They know when to ask for help, which is important.

One thing that has impressed me right from the start is that support and training of the parents is given a high priority at Vidya Sagar. I have come to realise since working at Vidya Sagar how vital this is and I am sure it is an area in which we could improve in the UK. Since doing the Transdisciplinary training the core team have been able to give programmes which fit into the daily routine of the child and their family, and so the therapy programmes are more purely ways of handling their children, rather than treatment programmes carried out at specific times. Also, because some of the staff that have undergone the Transdisciplinary training are parents of children with special needs, they have added a more personal aspect to the training approach, again contributing to its success.

Personally, I have learnt a great deal from being involved in this project. Approaching each child from the life roles angle reduces the tendency to see them as a medical condition, and to address their needs as an individual, and member of a family. I have seen how little carry over there can be from the physiotherapy room to the child's life if treatment principles are not integrated into a daily routine. From working more closely with the parents I have also begun to understand more clearly the issues that they are facing.

I definitely see the relevance of training individuals in all three therapy disciplines, particularly in a country such as India where there are so many different issues to consider. The needs of families differ in many ways from families in developed countries. Rural locations in India have problems of both limited access to education and limited access to medical facilities, and also the housing and lifestyles of the families mean that they have very different needs and expectations from people living in a developed country. Poor families living in cities have similar problems. Of course, any family will benefit from having less appointments to attend and less treatment programmes to carry out at home.

In conclusion, I can see the relevance of this way of working, particularly in a country such as India, and from my experience at Vidya Sagar, I can see that it is possible to develop this way of working. My concerns are regarding maintaining the quality of the training, the team that are going to continue to run this course will need to make sure that their own skills are kept up to date and continue to develop their own expertise. Continuing to work closely with the medical team will ensure that the Transdisciplinary workers maximise the advice and input they can give to the families with which they work.

Rachel Strang—Occupational Therapist

Having recently completed an M.Sc. in Community Disability Studies at the Institute of Child Health in London, and with twelve years' experience working as a paediatric occupational therapist, I arrived in India keen to find work which would allow me to progress my ideas about using a more comprehensive or holistic approach when working with children with disabilities. To move away from a medical model or approach to treatment and aim towards following a more social model. Involvement in developing the Transdisciplinary training at Vidya Sagar gave me an opportunity to do just that. Not only was I able to use my own experience and knowledge to develop the skills of others, but I also had opportunity to work closely with people who had different professional and cultural backgrounds than myself. We all had a common aim, to provide the best possible service for the disabled children with whom we were working. Together we had a wealth of experience and it was sharing knowledge with the core team members and the other Action Health Trainers which allowed us to evolve this new concept of a Transdisciplinary worker.

Towards the beginning of my time at Vidya Sagar, I talked to the core team about the principles and philosophy of occupational therapy as it is practised today. I had felt that the expectations of what is done by an occupational therapist expressed by the core team had been very narrow, with an emphasis on hand therapy and art and craft work. After I had explained the much broader role of an occupational therapist from my perspective, an interesting comment was made in reply. It was felt that the role that I had described was, in fact, very similar to the role of a special educator. I think that this illustrates clearly the enormous overlap in roles when working with children with special needs. Although there are still many things which a special educator can learn from an occupational therapist, and vice versa, the development of one professional who can amalgamate both roles was clearly not only feasible but advantageous in terms of reducing numbers of staff involved with one child and aiding communication.

Developing the occupational therapy aspect of the Transdisciplinary course was very much a process of learning together. We were able to explore various ideas and concepts and discuss their relevance to working with children with special needs. I felt that my main role was to outline some of the principles of occupational therapy, the process of assessment, treatment and remediation. Also, to discuss some of the theories which originate in the disciplines of neuro-physiology, psychology and the social sciences and which provide a foundation for modern approaches to treatment. I was dependent on the core team members to find ways of making this theoretical framework relevant and realistic in their own work settings, and ultimately in the work settings of those Transdisciplinary workers to whom they will be offering training. It is now two years since I completed my work at Vidya Sagar and returned to the UK. Looking back on my experience I feel very positive about what we were able to achieve together. I am encouraged to hear from my colleagues in Chennai that core team members are now using a Transdisciplinary approach. Aims and objectives are being set for the children covering broad range of therapeutic needs, and activities are being used which will help skill development in a number of areas at the same time. My hope is that the concept of Transdisciplinary working will continue to be developed and evolved both within Vidya Sagar and by professionals from further afield who have been able to receive the Transdisciplinary training.

Ruth Duncan—Speech Therapist

I came to the project at Vidya Sagar after having already spent three years working in India. My experience had been in rural community based rehabilitation, where I had been responsible for providing training and support on communication disability to a large team of disability workers working in upwards of 100 villages across a vast geographical area. These multi-rehab workers were responsible for looking at all the disability and health related needs of the children with whom they were working, a concept similar to that of the Transdisciplinary worker. The key difference though was that whereas the multi-rehab worker is concerned with children and adults with all types of disability, the goal of the Vidya Sagar programme was to develop individuals with expertise specifically in cerebral palsy and multiple disabilities. My interest was therefore how, and indeed whether, it would be possible to train the core team to the level required for them to become competent and confident in handling all therapy and education aspects of these complex children.

I found a team with a great deal of enthusiasm and practical experience. They had some theoretical knowledge already, but this required consolidating in order for them to have a firm foundation on which to build their knowledge and understanding. Since they had all been working with children with cerebral palsy for so long, they were able to relate well, and had plenty of opportunity to put new concepts into practice in the Centre. It was ideal running the communication training alongside the occupational therapy input since some of the approaches coincide and there was obvious interrelation between areas of sensory development, feeding difficulties and so on. I did feel at times as though we were expecting the core team to take on too much information in one stretch, and it was difficult for them just in terms of time to put all aspects into practice. In order to tackle this problem, we have reduced the depth of input in some topics for the Transdisciplinary training course as it now exists, with the emphasis on practical aspects and inter-linking between the three therapies. Since the team had already had input on physiotherapy, they were keen to look at ways in which targets and activities could be integrated, and came up with some imaginative ways of doing this. The most exciting and challenging part of the training came when we looked at Transdisciplinary case studies. Communication takes place in all situations and at all times of the day, but all too often speech and language therapy is seen as a series of exercises carried out in isolation with little carry over or relevance to the child's life. It was rewarding therefore to see the core team take therapy activities out of the 'speech room' and into the child's everyday environment, whether that be the classroom, the physiotherapy room, the sensory room or even the corridor at lunchtime. Understanding of positioning and sensory difficulties helped with handling the complex communication needs of children who are unable to speak or move their body to any great extent. In some cases, the goals for children completely changed and it was rewarding to see the core team take on these challenges as their understanding and confidence grew.

Personally, I learnt a great deal about areas in which I previously had little experience, particularly sensory deficits and movement. The process of supporting the core team in setting Transdisciplinary goals and therapy activities helped me to further develop my own analysis and goal setting skills. The staff at Vidya Sagar take it for granted that parents are at the centre of the intervention process. Seeing this in action reinforced my belief that parents must be key to anything we do with children, if we are to empower both child and family to handle the disability and sustain the child's development. Over and over again I found myself both amazed and humbled by the commitment of all the staff at Vidya Sagar. Working alongside Rachel and Katy helped me with my own professional development, in the areas of working with cerebral palsy and also as a trainer.

I believe strongly that the concept of the Transdisciplinary worker is of great relevance to the field of cerebral palsy and multiple disability. These individuals have needs that are varied and complex and which cannot be separated out. Intervention must be holistic with the individual at the centre. An integrated approach is also more meaningful for the caregiver and enables them to make better sense of the child's needs. Equally, in a country like India where allocated resources are spread thinly and many do not have access to professionals, the Transdisciplinary worker is of benefit in many settings including rural areas, community programmes in cities and schools where disabled children have been included into the mainstream. In order to maintain the quality and usefulness of the Transdisciplinary worker though, it is critical that they are kept in touch with therapists and other health professionals. Through this contact, they can update their knowledge and skills, and access specialist opinions and input. I hope that continuing professional development will be built into the training of all Transdisciplinary workers to ensure that the input provided to children, families and the broader community is appropriate and of maximum benefit.

9

Reflections and Recommendations

Having come to a point where this concept is now a way of working at Vidya Sagar , the team who have been involved in the project have been able to reflect on some of the issues that have arisen during the past four years. This final chapter will look at these issues and also discuss the possible future for this concept.

Criticisms of this concept

As mentioned earlier in this book, the main criticism of this concept has been that the idea of training one person in all disciplines is too much for one individual to handle; the idea that they will become 'Jack of all trades, master of none.' The team who are now working as Transdisciplinary workers do not think that that is the case. The point to understand here is that they have trained in the areas of therapy related to children with neurological conditions only. Also the level of their knowledge is not so specialised as the individual therapists, it is on a more Need To Know basis. The key for Transdisciplinary workers is to be able to recognise when to refer to the individual therapists for more advice. Also, they now have a greater understanding of medical jargon that enables them to better understand the advice given by the medical team.

As stated in Chapter 1, Poonam, as a parent, was expected to take on board all the information from all the therapists. I am sure many therapists working in the field of disability can recall parents who have developed an enormous amount of understanding about their child's condition has and coped with all their needs on a daily basis.

This leads to another criticism voiced about the concept—the fact that developing a Transdisciplinary worker encroaches upon the roles of the health professionals. In fact, the opposite of this should be true. By having these individuals trained in the basics of therapy for neurological conditions, the therapists themselves are freer to develop more specific expertise on more complex issues and cases.

At this point it should also be identified that the needs of a developing country such as India are very different from the West. There are many areas of the country where people have little or no access to the whole medical team and so these Transdisciplinary workers are a vital source of advice and support. This model hopes to empower people who work in areas where there is no multidisciplinary team.

A few people have questioned the difference between a multi-rehab worker and a Transdisciplinary worker. The Transdisciplinary Management Course developed by Vidya Sagar is primarily an advanced level course for graduates and post-graduates with at least two years' experience, who are already specialists in the field of speech therapy, physiotherapy, occupational therapy or special education. This course gives a holistic approach to handling children with cerebral palsy and associated conditions, which is based on neuro-developmental therapy. It enhances the management skills and training skills of the professional, adding to their existing skills. It also covers the communication and sensory issues of children with autism spectrum disorder. In contrast to this, the courses run by RCI, namely, Diploma in Community Based Rehabilitation for Disabled, Diploma in Multi Rehabilitation Worker Course, and Masters in Rehabilitation Science, are for first level field workers with a basic education background till the 12th grade. These courses cover aspects of various disabilities and conditions, including management, assessment and programme planning, exclusively for community implementation. The courses do not provide the trainees with skills of independent handling and programme planning.

One further criticism that was brought up by the medical team involved in this project was that the level of knowledge in areas such as anatomy should be more. As doctors and therapists, many months and years are spent studying the minute details of anatomy and so the few days spent on anatomy in the Transdisciplinary course will obviously seem very inadequate in comparison. The point here is that the Transdisciplinary course is not aiming to produce doctors and therapists. As already stated, the key is for these Transdisciplinary workers to know the basics and, most importantly, understand when to refer. The team at Vidya Sagar, who between them have many years of experience working with people with neurological conditions, feel that, contrary to this need to have more training in anatomy, what is actually needed is more training in nurturing. What they have noticed is that as these children become adults, when there is little, if any, role left for the doctors and other members of the medical team, these individuals still have problems fitting into society. These problems arise not only from society's views of people with disabilities, but also from the individuals themselves. Often they have lived in a very protected environment, and so to function in the harsh reality of the 'big wide world' can be extremely difficult for them.

One of the beliefs underlying this whole concept is that people with multiple disabilities need to be treated as people rather than a series of medical conditions. There comes a point where doctors and therapists have no more to offer these people, but, as stated, these people still have needs. A Transdisciplinary worker looks at all the areas of a child's development and prioritises their needs according to age-appropriate life roles. Further understanding of how to help these children to develop into emotionally mature adults would therefore be a more useful addition to the training module. If you were to directly compare the approach of the multidisciplinary team to that of a Transdisciplinary worker, it could be said that the multidisciplinary team prioritise the child's needs according to their field, whereas a Transdisciplinary worker prioritises according to the child.

The future for this concept

Quite a lot has already been said about the relevance of this way of working in rural areas in developing countries. Within cities, however, where there is more ready access to the multidisciplinary team, it may be argued that the need for this type of a worker is not so great.

However, there is the issue of inclusion to take into consideration. The issue of inclusion is still debated by many people, particularly for those children who are 'profoundly disabled'. This is where people with cerebral palsy really suffer. They become marginalised even within the disability sector as they cannot access the rights given to them under the People With Disabilties Act 1995 or the education policy which proclaims 'Education for all'.

In India, every person must have a disability certificate certifying a certain percentage of disability by a doctor. Classifications exist for people with disabilities in the areas of:

- Locomotor
- Vision
- Hearing
- Intellectual functioning

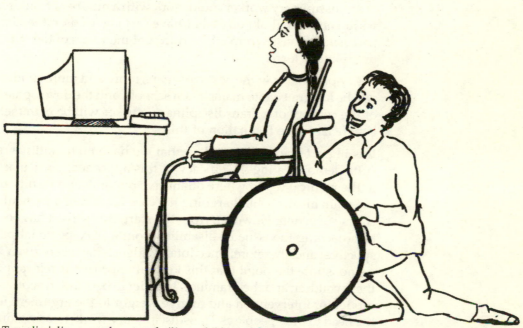

Transdisciplinary workers can facilitate children to fit into the mainstream classroom.

Therefore, a person with cerebral palsy may easily fall under more than one category. There is major confusion then as to what the percentage disability should be. For example, a person who is quadriplegic will have 80–90 per cent disability. Then, if there is an added low vision problem, the disability may be 60 per cent. In total therefore, this person, has more than 100 per cent disability and will of course be termed profoundly disabled. The fact that this person could be cognitively high functioning is another matter.

These individuals are then still sent to special schools, where it is unlikely that they will have the opportunity to undertake examinations.

Transdisciplinary workers, who understand the global needs of these children, would be able to facilitate them to fit into the mainstream classroom. Again, the fact that the Transdisciplinary worker has knowledge in all three areas of therapy as well as education would mean that the class teacher need only liaise with one person rather than a whole medical team. In large classes, such as there are in mainstream schools in India, this time saving would be invaluable. Also important is the fact that one Transdisciplinary worker could work with a number of children within one school, although they have varying needs, rather than necessitating visits from all the different members of the multi-disciplinary team.

It is hoped that over the next few years, more and more children will be integrated into mainstream schools, and the development of the concept of a Transdisciplinary worker will be extremely beneficial in the facilitation of this.

It is likely to be commented on that we have no quantitive results demonstrating the efficacy of this approach, particularly in the medical world where quantitive research and results are the main means behind arguing the case for taking a particular course of action. However, from the start, this project has been approaching the issue of disability from a very personal perspective, and therefore, anecdotal evidence has been given to demonstrate the point that this kind of approach is relevant to these children and their families. In order to become an accepted model for intervention and to give weight to the argument for the need to train people as Transdisciplinary workers, some kind of quantitive study will undoubtedly need to be done.

However, many measuring tools used to assess the efficiency of input for children with disability have specific measures, such as: Is the child able to get up to standing independently? From the perspective of people who have been involved in this project, we would like to ask, does the child need to stand independently? What can they do once they have stood up? We would like to know the answer to more vague questions like: Does the child have a role within the family? Do the parents feel able to manage their child confidently?

Developing a realistic and relevant measure to research this method of intervention and compare it to other models of intervention would be the next step to take to give weight to the arguments for training more Transdisciplinary workers and then recognising them as professionals within their own right.

Conclusions

This concept of a Transdisciplinary worker is still evolving, and as more people go on to be trained in this way, it will be even more clear what the training needs are for such professionals. The idea is evolving to meet the changing needs of society, and although this project has taken place in a developing country, where the issues faced are different from those of a western country, the benefits of working in this way would also work in a more developed country.

This concept enables professionals to work in partnership with the person with a disability and her/his family and prioritise the needs of the child or adult more appropriately by looking at life roles. Through looking at life roles, persons with disabilities are helped to develop their own and their family's expectations for independence and also take a more active role, both at home and in society. As stated earlier in this chapter, we feel that learning how to help these individuals to become emotionally mature, where they can take success and failure, is the direction we need to consider when developing this concept further.

In conclusion, we believe that a Transdisciplinary worker, who understands the needs of a person with a neurological disability more clearly, will be able to provide the person with realistic and achievable goals for her/his life, and work closely with the parents and help them to understand their child better.

As Poonam, from her viewpoint as a mother, puts it:

> It is very liberating for a parent to see a child as a person rather than many medical conditions!

Appendix

Initial proposed curriculum for the physiotherapy/occupational therapy module—1999

Normal musculoskeletal anatomy	2 days
Normal neuroanatomy	1 day
Normal neurophysiology	2 days
Normal musculoskeletal physiology	2 days
Normal physical and motor child development	2 days
Mechanism of normal tone	2 days
Mechanism of normal movement	2 days
Causes/types of cerebral palsy	1 day
Clinical features of cerebral palsy	1 day
Aims of physiotherapy in the management of the child with cerebral palsy	2 days
Aims of occupational therapy in the management of the child with cerebral palsy	2 days
Subjective/objective assessment of the child with cerebral palsy	5 days
Introduction to neuro developmental therapy concept	3 days
Conductive education in the management of the child with cerebral palsy	3 days
Contractures	
causes and prevention	1 day
assessment	2 days
management	3 days
Post-operative therapy following corrective surgery	1 day
Treatment techniques in the management of hypertonicity and hypotonicity	4 days

Treatment techniques to develop the functional development of the child with cerebral palsy	3 days
Treatment techniques to develop static and dynamic equilibrium/balance reactions in the child with cerebral palsy	3 days
Importance of early stimulation in the child with cerebral palsy	2 days
Positioning the child with cerebral palsy	2 days
Use of aids and appliances for positioning the child with cerebral palsy	2 days
Biomechanics of normal gait	1 day
Gait re-education	2 days
Use of aids and appliances for improving mobility in children with cerebral palsy	2 days
Treatment techniques to develop self-help skills	3 days
Treatment techniques to develop hand function	3 days
Wheelchairs	2 days

Poliomyelitis
    causes, clinical features secondary problems
        assessment
        management   3 days

Muscular dystrophy
    causes, clinical features, secondary problems
        assessment
        management   1/2 day

Spina bifida
    causes, clinical features, secondary problems
        assessment
        management   1 day

Talipes equinovarus
    assessment
    management   1 day

Arthrogryposis
    assessment
    management   1/2 day

Contraindications in management of above conditions   2 days

Hydrotherapy	1 day
Riding for the disabled	1 day
Use of toys in the management of disability	1 day
Group therapy/creative movement/individual therapy—interlinking	1 day
Vocational rehabilitation	1 day
Documentation and goal setting	1 day
Total	**80 days**

Communication therapy training curriculum

Vidya Sagar/Action Health 2000–2001

1. Introduction module

- Interactive approach to communication therapy
- Child and adult styles
- Peer interactions

2. Assessment and treatment procedures

- Factors involved in assessment
- Initial screening assessment
- Use of language and interaction—interactive curriculum
- Receptive and expressive language—Derbyshrine Language-Scheme, STASS

- Speech

  - articulation
  - phonology
  - dysarthria

- Language disorder

  - understanding and use of semantics, morphology & syntax
  - pragmatics

- Fluency and voice—overview of assessment and management techniques

3. Alternative and augmentative communication

- Introduce   Reasons for AAC use
  Types of AAC user
  Types of AAC
- Assessment   Basic Skills
  Confirmation and negation
  Positioning
  Scanning
  Symbol assessment
  Language assessment
  Access
- Implementation Introduction, ongoing development and review generalisation—a team approach.
- Pragmatics of AAC Role of listener
  Characteristics of communication with an AAC device

4. Feeding

5. Autism and related disorder

6. Hearing impairment

- Anatomy, causes and types of loss
- Role of medical and audio-logical professionals
- Methods of learning/teaching
- Auditory training and developing listening skills
- Speech reading
- Speech and language development
- Total communication

7. Rounding up, putting all together and evaluation

Vidya Sagar

Occupational therapy skills course communication

Aims

- Course participants will be able to incorporate good occupational therapy principles and practice into their everyday working situations with children with special needs.

- Participants will be able to understand, analyse and evaluate occupational therapy principles and practice and convey this knowledge to others through formal teaching sessions as well as during everyday practice.

Curriculum

Occupational therapy principles and practice

- Introduction
- Definitions and history
- Models of practice
- Task analysis
- Assessment and goal setting

Occupational tasks

- Activities of daily living
- Work and education
- Play

Physical skills and functional ability

- Seating and wheelchairs
- Hand function and fine motor skills
- Assessment
- Aids and adaptations

Perceptual skills and functional ability

- Sensory stimulation
- Sensory integration
- Bobath
- Motor learning
- Application to functional tasks with children

Neurodevelopment and motor learning approaches to treatment

- Sensory stimulation
- Sensory integration
- Bobath
- Motor learning
- Application to functional tasks with children

Transferring OT (occupational therapy) skills to others

- Course review
- Training parents
- Using professional OTs as a resource
- Teaching methods

Expectation

- The course will be divided up into six modules. Each module will cover a different aspect of occupational therapy related to working with children with special needs.
- At the beginning of each module, objective will be set by all the course participants together with the course tutor. Areas covered in the objectives should include skills, knowledge and attitude.
- Each module will be evaluated by the course participants. The purpose of evaluation will include reviewing the objectives set together, identifying the main topics taught and discussing their relevance, identifying the teaching methods used and discussing their effectiveness.
- For each module participants will complete one assignment, to be handed in on the Monday following the completion of each module.

All students will be expected to participate in class activities such as presentation, case studies, fact-finding missions (such as looking up information in library) and critical reading, as well as attending lectures and one to one sessions.

Transdisciplinary course content – January 2004

Introductory module   44 hours
Life roles—introduction and analysis
Perspective to disability and education
Introduction to Transdisciplinary philosophy
Transdisciplinary approaches
Introduction to the learning process
Introduction to special needs
Introduction to cerebral palsy
Task analysis

Normal development module   24 hours
Introduction to child development
Foetal development

Normal postures and movements
Development of hand function
Automatic and voluntary movements
Speech and language development
Normal eating and drinking
Play

Anatomy and physiology module   18 hours
Joints—anatomy and ranges of movement
Muscles—anatomy and action
Muscle physiology
Neuroanatomy and neurophysiology—CNS/PNS/ANS

Management module   190 hours
Neurodevelopmental Management—Introduction, assessment
    and techniques
Postural management
Early intervention
Sensory integration—Analysis and application
Hand function assessment and management
Praxis—definition, understanding and management of problems
Communication:
    Interactive curriculum
    Social curriculum
Derbyshire language scheme
Assessment, analysis and techniques for management
AAC
Language disorders—analysis and strategies for management
Multiple disabilities:
    Cerebral palsy with visual impairment
    Cerebral palsy with hearing impairment
    Cerebral palsy—deaf and blind

Eating and drinking in children with cerebral palsy
Cognitive assessment
Mental retardation and task analysis
Functional behaviour analysis
Perception and reading, writing and maths
Learning disability—characteristics, assessment and strategies
Teaching skills
Autism—assessment and strategies
Multiple intelligence—understanding and application
Other conditions—differentiation from cerebral palsy, implications,
    basic management
Gait analysis—application of orthotics and walking aids

Contractures—indications for surgery, medication and orthotics
Pre and post operative therapy

Transdisciplinary management
Goal setting
Programme planning
Classroom management
Planning instruction
Evaluation

Documentation
Adults with special needs
Vocational opportunities
Independence
Relating to life roles

Practical Time   54 hours

Total   330 hours

Addresses

Vidya Sagar
1 Ranjith Road
Kotturpuram
Chennai 600 035
Tamil Nadu
INDIA

Skillshare International
126 New Walk
Leicester
LE1 7 JA
UK

Bibliography

Allen, William T. 1989. *Read My Lips. Its My Choice*. Minnesota Governor's Planning Council on Developmental Disabilities.

Ayres, Jane. 1996. *Sensory Integration and the Child*. Western Psychological Services.

Bernthal, Jone and Nicholas W. Bankson. 2004. *Articulation and Phonological Disorders*. Allyn and Bacon.

Cooke, Jackie and Diana Williams. 1987. *Working with Children's Language: Intervention Strategies for Therapy*. Communication Skill Builders.

Costello, Janis. 1984. *Speech Disorder in Children: Recent Advances*. College Hill Press.

Detheridge, Tina and Mike Detheridge. 2002. *Literacy Through Symbols: Improving Access for Children and Adults*. David Fulton Publishers Ltd.

Dormans, John P. and Louis Pellegrino. 1998. *Caring for Children with Cerebral Palsy. A Team-based Approach*. Brookes Publishing Company.

Dorothy E., Penso. 1992. *Perceptual Motor Difficulties: Theory and Strategies to Help Children, Adolescents and Adults*. Stanley Thornes Publishers Ltd.

E. Bruce, Goldstein. 1996. *Sensation and Perception*. Wadsworth Publishing.

Finnie, Nancie R et al. 1974. *Handling the Young Cerebral Palsied Child at Home*. Butterworth Heineman.

Illingworth, Ronald S. 1983. *The Normal Child*. Churchill Livingstone.

Karanth, Pratibha et al. 1999. 'With a Little Bit of Help: Early Language Training Manual.'

Kashyap, Tripura. 'Handbook for Special Educators, Therapists and Parents, Therapeutic Movement Activities with Disabilities.'

Kaufman, Douglas, David M. Moss and Terry A. Osborn. 2004. *Beyond the Boundaries: A Transdisciplinary Approach to Learning and Teaching*. Greenwood Publishing Group.

Kranowitz, Carol. 1998. *The Out of Sync Child: Recognizing and Coping with Sensory Integration Dysfunction*. Penguin Books.

Lynch, Charlotte and Julia Kidd. 1999. *Early Communication Skills*. Speechmark Publishing Ltd.

Marianne, Frostig. 1963. *Development Test of Visual Perception*. Consulting Psychologists Press.

McCurtin, Arlene and G. Murray. 2000. The Manual of AAC Assessment. Winslow Press.

McCurtin, Arlene. 1997. *Manual of Paediatric Feeding Practice*. Speechmark Publishing Ltd.

Orelove, Fred P. and Dick Sobsey. 1996. *Educating Children with Multiple Disabilities: A Transdisciplinary Approach*. Brookes Publishing Company.

Porter, Gayle and Jann Kirkland. *Integrated Augmentative and Alternative Communication into Group Programmes: Utilizing the Principle of Conductive Education*. A Handbook.

Rowland, Charity and Philip Schweigert. 1993. *The Early Communication Process Using Microswitch Technology*. Communication Skill Builders.

Sher, Barbara and Janet Young. 1992. *Extraordinary Play with Ordinary Things: Recycling Everyday Materials to Build Motor Skills*. Adams Media Corp.

Smith, Millie. 1998. 'Joseph's Coat: People Teaming in Transdisciplinary Ways.' Retrieved August 15, 2001, from Texas School for the Blind and Visually Impaired Website: http://www.tsbvi. edu/Outreach/seehear/spring98/joseph.html.

Stuart, Lynn, Felicity Wright, Sue Grigor and Alison Howey. 2002. *Spoken Language Difficulties: Practical Strategies and Activities for Teachers and Other Professionals*. David Fulton Publishers Ltd.

Sussman, Fern. 1999. *More than Words. Helping Parents Promote Communication and Social Skills in Children with Autism Spectrum Disorder*. Hanen Centre.

Tortora, Gerard J. & Nicholas P. Anagnostakos and Elaine Nicpon-Marieb. 2000. *Principles of Anatomy and Physiology*. John Wiley & Sons.

Trombly, Catherine A. 2002. *Occupational Therapy for Physical Dysfunction*. Lippincott Williams & Wilkins Publish.

Trott, Maryann Codby, Marci K. Laurel and Susan L. Windeck. 1993. *Sensibilities: Understanding Sensory Integration*. Therapy Skill Builders.

Turner, Ann. 2002. *Occupational Therapy and Physical Dysfunction: Principle, Skills and Practice*. Churchill Livingstone.

Warrick, Anne and Sudha Kaul. *Augmentative Communication for Children and Young Adults with Severe Speech Disorders*. Indian Institute of Cerebral Palsy, Spastics Society of Eastern India.

Watson, Linda R., Catherine Lord, Bruce Schaffer and Eric Schopler. 1988. *Teaching Spontaneous Communication to Autistic and Developmentally Handicapped Children*. Irvington Publishers.

Weitzman, Elaine and Janice Greenber. 2002. *Learning Language and Loving It*: *A Guide to Promoting Children's Social, Language and Literacy Development*. Hanen Centre.

Williams, Diana. 1995. *Early Listening Skills*. Speechmark Publishing Ltd.

Winterton, Tara. 1992. 'Communication with Children: A Language Training Manual. Unpublished.

Wirth, Marian Jenks. 1976. *Teachers Handbook of Children Games: A Guide to Developing Perceptual Motor Skills*. Parker Publishing Company.

Wirz, Sheila and Sandy Winyard. 1993. *Hearing and Communication Disorders*. Macmillan.

Wood, David, Heather Wood, Amanda Griffiths and Ian Howarth. 1992. *Teaching and Talking with Deaf Children*. John Wiley & Sons Ltd.

Research Papers

- Development of sitting ability, assessment of children with a motor handicap and prescription of appropriate seating systems by E.M. Green and R.L. Nelham—Rehabilitation Engineering Unit. Chailey Heritage Lewes, UK
- The Sacred Pad—Description of its clinical use in seating by C.M. Mulcahy and T.E. Pountney—Rehabilitation Engineering Unit. Chailey Heritage Lewes, UK

Index

About the Author

Kate Tebbett is a senior paediatric physiotherapist. She has worked as a community paediatric physiotherapist in Northamptonshire, Leicestershire and Cumbria in the United Kingdom. Kate Tebbett worked with Vidya Sagar, a Chennai-based NGO, from 1999 to 2004 as a Health Trainer placed by Skillshare International. She helped develop a model for training special educators to provide treatment to people, especially children, with a range of disabilities. Kate, her husband and their two young boys live in the Yorkshire Dales, UK.

The team which developed the Transdisciplinary approach described in this book included Rachel Strang, Ruth Duncan Patil, Kate Tebbett, and Poonam Natarajan and her team. The work was the result of a joint initiative of Vidya Sagar, a Chennai-based NGO, and Skillshare International, a UK charity.